CHICAGO > EAT!

WHAT'S INSIDE

TOP PICKS
- 4 French and Contemporary
- 6 Italian and Pizza
- 8 Latin
- 10 Asian
- 12 Cheap Chow
- 14 Outdoor Dining
- 16 Local Favorites

WHERE TO EAT WHEREVER YOU
- 20 Magnificent Mile and
- 30 Gold Coast and Old To
- 36 River North
- 40 Loop
- 44 Randolph Market and
- 48 Greektown and West L
- 52 South Loop and Chinat
- 56 Pilsen and Little Italy
- 60 Bucktown and Wicker
- 66 Lincoln Park
- 72 Lakeview
- 78 Roscoe Village and Nor
- 82 Lincoln Square
- 86 Uptown and Anderson
- 92 Index

TOP PICKS

Sometimes you pick a restaurant because it's near something else. When your meal is the focus of your evening (or your afternoon), check out the restaurants on the next pages. Each ranks among the city's top picks in its category, and each is well worth a trip from the other end of town.

WHAT WILL IT COST?
Prices are indicated according to the cost of entrées at dinner:

$	$15 and under
$$	$16 -$24
$$$	$25-32
$$$$	$33 and up

When waiters recite the daily specials, always ask about prices before ordering. You can use AE, D, MC, V—American Express, Diner's Club, MasterCard or Visa—in all but the smallest restaurants in this book.

WHERE > CHICAGO > EAT!

FRENCH AND CONTEMPORARY

ALINEA The sleek and futuristic interior of this restaurant proves itself fully the equal of the spectacular 12- and 24-course tasting menus of artistically rendered experimental dishes from chef Grant Achatz.
Lincoln Park
$$$$

AVENUES Cutting-edge cuisine (think lavender-crusted squab with garlic marmalade) meets lush, traditional surroundings at this Peninsula Hotel restaurant.
Magnificent Mile
$$$$

CHARLIE TROTTER'S This internationally acclaimed restaurant put Chicago on the culinary map with its stunning eight-course dégustation menus and wine pairings.
Lincoln Park
$$$$

MOTO If you think eating should be an adventure, chef Homaro Cantu's restaurant is for you: His whimsical, experimental dishes might include anything from edible paper to soup-filled syringes.
Randolph Market and River West
$$$$

SIGNATURE ROOM AT THE 95TH Jaw-dropping panoramic views upstage even the good contemporary American fare at this restaurant atop the John Hancock Building.
Gold Coast
$$$

TRU Chef Rick Tramonto's progressive French cuisine is impeccably presented in a spacious, sensuous dining room filled with contemporary art.
Magnificent Mile
$$$$

WHERE FRENCH AND CONTEMPORARY

ITALIAN AND PIZZA

MIA FRANCESCA Famously noisy and bustling, Mia Francesca is a longtime Chicago favorite for its consistently good Italian food and high-energy buzz.
Lakeview
$$

PIZZERIA UNO The birthplace of crusty, cheesy, deep-dish Chicago pizza, is always crowded but well worth the wait.
Magnificent Mile
$$

SPACCA NAPOLI Authentic Neapolitan-style pizza is served piping hot in a contemporary, upbeat dining room.
Lincoln Square
$

SPIAGGIA One of the city's finest Italian restaurants, Spiaggia is in a prime location overlooking the Oak Street Beach.
Magnificent Mile
$$$$

TERRAGUSTO Homemade pastas, fresh ingredients, and a seasonal menu bring the food at this low-key café as close to genuine Italian cooking as it gets.
Roscoe Village
$$

TUFANO'S VERNON PARK TAP Generations of Chicagoans have enjoyed the filling southern Italian cooking at this popular Little Italy destination.
Little Italy
$$

LATIN

BOMBON The Mexican and European pastries, cookies, and breads at this cheery and eye-catching bakery are nothing short of luscious.
Pilsen
$

CARNIVALE An enormous, stylish spectacle of a dining room sets the stage for an adventurous menu of pan-Latin fare.
River West
$$–$$$

CUERNAVACA This venerable neighborhood favorite owes its longevity to its authentic Mexican cuisine and colorful setting.
Pilsen
$

FRONTERA GRILL/TOPOLOBAMPO A festive, stylish celebration of the best of regional Mexican cuisine, these sister restaurants serve the kind of Mexican fare you don't often find north of the border.
Magnificent Mile
$$

MAS The Wicker Park dining scene is always changing, but the contemporary Latin dishes and fantastic margaritas at Mas keep it crowded and trendy.
Wicker Park
$$$

NACIONAL 27 Everyone comes for the ambitious Central and South American menu—but inevitably, they take a turn on the dance floor and salsa until the early morning hours.
River North
$$$

ASIAN

HAI YEN The number of Vietnamese restaurants on Argyle Street is head-spinning, but with a huge selection, reasonable prices, and excellent staff, Hai Yen stands out.
Uptown
$

LAO SZE CHUAN Chinese-food aficionados rank this busy Chinatown spot among the best in the city for southwestern Chinese fare.
Chinatown
$$

LE LAN Delicate orchids grace every table at this calm, civilized oasis of well-executed French-Asian cooking.
Magnificent Mile
$$$–$$$$

MARIGOLD Colorful, lofty, and cutting-edge without being pretentious, this excellent Indian restaurant is reason enough to make the trip to Uptown.
Uptown
$$

TANK SUSHI It may be chic and it may be clubby, but it's delightfully friendly nonetheless, and the small plates of sushi and Asian fare are delicious.
Lincoln Square
$$$

THAI CLASSIC An inexpensive weekend buffet, friendly service, and tasty Thai dishes draw diners to this icon-filled Clark Street restaurant.
Lakeview
$

CHEAP CHOW

AL's #1 ITALIAN BEEF The always-busy Italian beef and sausage joint on Taylor Street in Little Italy is a Chicago institution.
Little Italy
$

DINER GRILL After bars close in the city, night owls looking for grill grub head to this brightly lit trailer. It doesn't just mimic the '50s—it is the '50s.
North Center
$

FOODLIFE Many different cuisines are represented at this quick-service cafeteria-style dining room in Water Tower Place, Chicago's landmark shopping destination.
Gold Coast
$

NUEVO LÉON Colorful, lively, and friendly, Nuevo Léon is also one of the city's best bets for authentic Mexican cuisine.
Pilsen
$

PODHALANKA POLKSA RESTAURACJA One of Chicago's best-kept secrets for filling Polish food. It's in the heart of the city's former "Polish Broadway."
Wicker Park
$

17-WEST AT THE BERGHOFF The downstairs café in this revamped Chicago classic serves some of the best deli sandwiches you'll find around downtown.
Loop
$$

WHERE **CHEAP CHOW**

OUTDOOR DINING

CAFÉ SELMARIE The plaza at this restaurant in the heart of Lincoln Square evokes the pleasantly buzzing pedestrian zones of European cities.
Lincoln Square
$–$$

FLATWATER Flatwater's broad river-front patio, just below the Clark Street bridge, delivers sweeping views of the downtown landscape.
River North
$–$$

NOMI In the seventh-floor garden of this Park Hyatt restaurant, birch trees and lush landscaping, slate floors, and a small pond create the perfect little cocoon for light meals and cocktails.
Gold Coast & Old Town
$$$$

NORTHSIDE BAR AND GRILL
A greenhouse-style dining space and patio make this hip grill serving burgers, salads, and drinks ideal for people-watching.
Bucktown & Wicker Park
$$

RESI'S BIERSTUBE
One of Chicago's oldest beer gardens, shaded with old maple trees, is a delightful place for a stein of Germany's finest.
North Center
$

TIMO
The large and beautifully landscaped garden of the Halsted Street Italian restaurant is one of the city's most popular alfresco dining spots.
Randolph Market & River West
$$$

WHERE OUTDOOR DINING

LOCAL FAVORITES

ANN SATHER An institution in Lakeview (with a few branches around town), Ann Sather is known for its Swedish and American comfort food and completely indulgent cinnamon rolls.
Lakeview
$–$$

BILLY GOAT This burger-and-beer shrine to Chicago journalists, lurking just below the Magnificent Mile, may be grungy, but it's loaded with atmosphere.
Magnificent Mile
$

EARWAX This laid-back and relaxing Wicker Park café was a pioneer during the neighborhood's 1980s hipster transformation, and it remains popular for its breakfasts, veggie fare, burgers, and more.
Wicker Park
$

HOPLEAF Once lauded mainly for its stellar selection of Belgian beers, Hopleaf has also made a name for itself as the home of some of the best bar food in town.
Andersonville
$$

MACY'S WALNUT ROOM This dining room in the former Marshall Field's was one of the first in the United States in a department store, and a meal here is still a holiday-season tradition among Chicagoans.
Loop
$$–$$$

SAPORI The generous portions of pasta and other Italian fare and the hearty welcome that makes even newcomers feel like regulars are the draws at this locally loved trattoria.
Lincoln Park
$$

WHERE LOCAL FAVORITES

WHERE TO EAT WHEREVER YOU ARE

From the South Side to Wicker Park and Bucktown, from Old Town to the West Loop, Chicago is stuffed with restaurants in every cuisine and price category, from ethnic nooks to culinary showstoppers. Look in the pages that follow to find the best place to grab a bite—wherever you are

WHERE TO EAT WHEREVER YOU ARE

MAGNIFICENT MILE AND STREETERVILLE

Restaurants on Michigan Avenue are in this section if they're at Chicago Avenue or south. Those north of Chicago Avenue are in the Gold Coast and Old Town section.

- American
- Chinese
- European
- Italian
- Japanese
- French and Contemporary
- Latin
- Mediterranean
- Seafood
- Steak
- World

● **AVENUES** Critically acclaimed chef Graham Elliot Bowles heads the kitchen at this luxurious restaurant in the Peninsula Hotel. On the cutting-edge menu, look for lobster with sunchokes, kumquats, and vanilla; lavender-crusted squab with fiddlehead ferns and garlic marmalade; and bison with grits, chard, and persimmons. The space itself is traditional, with a golden-marble counter, gold satin curtains, light wood paneling, and a stellar view of the Magnificent Mile. 108 E Superior St, betw Michigan and Rush, 312/573-6754. No lunch; closed Sun and Mon. El: Red to Chicago. AE, D, DC, MC, V.
$$$$

● **BEN PAO** Pillars, waterfalls, and a stunning gold-and-red color scheme add Asian sophistication to this Cantonese restaurant. The menu gives a contemporary twist to retro dishes from moo goo gai pan (chicken-and-vegetable stir-fry) and lemon chicken to yu shian pork (shredded meat with oyster sauce) and shrimp fried rice. There's also a less formal satay bar and communal dining area known as the Hot Pot Café. Carryout and delivery are available.
52 W Illinois St, betw Dearborn and Clark, 312/222-1888. No lunch weekends. El: Red to Grand. AE, D, DC, MC, V.
$$$

● **BICE RISTORANTE** Tuscan cuisine has found a stylish, comfortable home in this space just off the Magnificent Mile. Look for classics such as prime-beef carpaccio, deep-fried calamari, and risotto with crab, mussels, calamari, and shrimp in tomato-herb sauce.
158 E Ontario St, betw Michigan and St Clair, 312/664-1474, bice.ws/BICE-CHICAGO.htm. El: Red to Chicago. AE, D, MC, V.
$$$

● **BILLY GOAT** Good greasy cheeseburger joints are a dime a dozen, but they rarely come with as much character as this legendary subterranean hole-in-the-wall. Smoke-yellowed photos of Chicago newspapermen and -women who boozed here way back when line the walls above the bar and low-budget seating area. The din of burger flippers shouting "cheezborger" drowns out the jukebox.

430 N Michigan Ave, lower level at North Water St, 312/222-1525, billygoattavern.com. El: Red to Grand. No credit cards.
$

● **BIN 36** A diverse crowd of nibblers from area businesses and the adjacent House of Blues hotel comes to this loft-like River North restaurant for the long communal dining table made from century-old barn wood and the creative seasonal American menu from chef John Caputo. The restaurant pours 50 wines by the glass, and the Carrera marble-topped cheese bar serves more than four dozen artisanal cheeses from around the world.
339 N Dearborn St, betw Kinzie and the river, 312/755-9463, bin36.com. Also serves breakfast. El: Red to Grand, Brown to Merchandise Mart. AE, D, MC, V.
$$–$$$

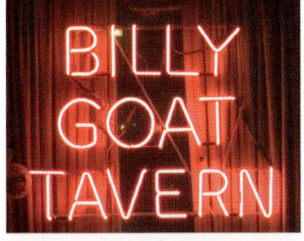

● **BRASSERIE JO** Under the direction of Alsatian chef-owner Jean Joho, this big room buzzes with expense-account diners enjoying regional French fare such as pepper-crusted swordfish and skate with capers and brown butter. 59 W Hubbard St, betw Dearborn and Clark, 312/595-0800, brasseriejo.com. No lunch. El: Brown, Purple to Merchandise Mart. AE, D, DC, MC, V.. $$–$$$

● **CAPITAL GRILLE** Dry-aged steaks, fresh seafood, and good wines are the strengths of this snazzy steakerie. The pretheater special runs a mere $40. 633 N St Clair St, at Ontario, 312/337-9400, thecapitalgrille.com. No lunch weekends. El: Red to Chicago. AE, D, DC, MC, V. $$$

● **CHICAGO CHOP HOUSE** Famous for huge USDA prime steaks, chops, and prime rib, this classy, masculine

restaurant is a Chicago superstar. The wine list includes 600 global selections; more than 40 are served by the glass. The piano bar starts weekdays at 5, weekends at 6. 60 W Ontario St, betw Dearborn and Clark, 312/787-7100, chicagochophouse.com. No lunch weekends. El: Red to Grand. AE, D, MC, V. $$$

● **DELACOSTA** In the glass-enclosed kitchen of this huge Latin supper club, James Beard Award-winning chef Douglas Rodriguez whips up creative plates like sugar-cane-skewered tuna, guava-molasses lamb ribs, and more. Designed by local hotshot Suhail (whose credits also include MTV's Real World Chicago house), the place also has a ceviche bar and a solarium lounge overlooking the Chicago River. 465 E Illinois St, at Peshtigo, 312/321-8930, delacostachicago.com. No lunch weekends. Bus: 65 to McClurg. AE, D, DC, MC, V. $$–$$$

FOX & OBEL

Billed as a fine-food emporium, this New York-style grocery carries only the best ingredients. Offerings include artisan breads and pastries, a butcher shop, fresh fish, a charcuterie department, a produce section, cheese, and an affordable café. You'll also find a diverse selection of wine, beer, and other beverages, plus hard-to-get culinary items. Catering, cooking classes, gift baskets, personal shopping, and delivery are all available.

401 E Illinois St, at McClurg 312/410-7301, fox-obel.com. Also serves breakfast. Bus: 65 to McClurg. AE, D, DC, MC, V.

$$–$$$

FRONTERA GRILL/TOPOLOBAMPO

Celebrity chef Rick Bayless teams with his wife, Deann, at one of the nation's most lauded Mexican restaurants, featuring made-from-scratch regional dishes in this colorful, buzzing restaurant duo—the elegant Topolobampo, and, next door, the more casual Frontera Grill, where the kitchen turns out spritely, mouth-filling street fare as well as creations such as halibut with tomatoes, chiles, cilantro, and olives.

445 N Clark St, 312/661-1434, frontera kitchens.com. Closed Sun and Mon. El: Red to Grand. AE, D, DC, MC, V.

$$

GINO'S EAST, THE ORIGINAL

A Chicago institution, the restaurant established in 1966 serves a legendary deep-dish pizza—a famously golden crust topped with chunky tomato sauce. You can also order your pizza with a thin crust, or go for pastas, salads, or sandwiches.

162 E Superior St, betw St Clair and Michigan, 312/266-3337, ginoseast .com. El: Red to Chicago. AE, D, MC, V. Also: 633 N Wells St, betw Ontario and Erie, River North, 312/943-1124. El: Brown, Purple to Chicago. AE, D, DC, MC, V. 2801 N Lincoln Ave, at Diversey, Lakeview, 773/327-3737. Bus: 11 to Diversey. AE, D, DC, MC, V.

$–$$

- **HARRY CARAY'S** Beloved Chicago Cubs sportscaster Harry Caray is the inspiration for this classic Italian steak joint, one of the city's best. Beneath walls of sports paraphernalia, a menu of prime well-executed steaks, chops, pastas, and more keeps meat lovers happy. You can also order from a more casual menu of sandwiches and salads at Harry's bar, which measures 60 feet and 6 inches in length—the distance from the pitcher's mound to home plate.
33 W Kinzie St, betw Dearborn and State, 312/828-0966, harrycarays.com. No lunch Sun (except for a sandwich cart in the bar). El: Red to Grand. AE, D, DC, MC, V.
$$–$$$

- **INDIAN GARDEN** Mughlai cooking is the focus here, but with a difference—chef Rawat's sauces are light and low in fat. The food is otherwise authentically prepared, in copper saucepans called patilas and in the traditional tandoor oven.
247 E Ontario St, 2nd floor, betw St Clair and Fairbanks, 312/280-4910. El: Red to Chicago. Also: 2548 W Devon Ave, betw Maplewood and Rockwell, Rogers Park, 773/338-2929. Bus: 155 to Rockwell. AE, D, DC, MC, V.
$$

- **THE KERRYMAN** Stone walls, mahogany accents, and leather booths decorate this Irish bar and restaurant in River North. Classics like fish-and-chips, shepherd's pie, and mac and cheese are on the menu, and in warm weather, you can do your noshing at tables set up outside.
661 N Clark St, 312/335-8121, thekerrymanchicago.com. El: Red to Chicago. AE, D, DC, MC, V.
$$

LAWRY'S THE PRIME RIB Roast prime rib of beef carved tableside is the specialty at this elegant restaurant just off the Magnificent Mile. Lawry's famous salad bowl, mashed potatoes, and Yorkshire pudding accompany the meal. There's also a nightly seafood selection with lobster tails.
100 E Ontario St, at Rush, 312/787-5000, lawrysonline.com. No lunch Sun. El: Red to Grand. AE, D, DC, MC, V.
$$–$$$

LE LAN This serenely minimalist spot represents the collaboration of celebrated chefs Roland Liccioni (Le Français, Les Nomades) and Arun Sampanthavivat (Arun's), and the menu is what you might expect, intermingling stylish French and contemporary Asian cuisines. Look for hot and cold Vietnamese spring rolls, duck breast with seared foie gras, and Asian-spiced beef tenderloin. Every Tuesday, a three-course meal goes for about $36.
749 N Clark St, 312/280-9100, lelan restaurant.com. No lunch; closed Sun. El: Red to Chicago. AE, DC, MC, V.
$$$–$$$$

MAMBO GRILL South American, Puerto Rican, Cuban, and Mexican influences mingle in this lively Latin room. The lunch menu includes enchiladas, flautas, quesadillas, and a selection of tortas (sandwiches). Dinner entrées range from Cuban- and Caribbean-style chicken and pork dishes to Argentine grill fare. The bar pours one of the city's largest selections of rums and tequilas.
412 N Clark St, betw Hubbard and Kinzie, 312/467-9797, mambogrill.com. No lunch Sat; closed Sun. El: Brown, Purple to Merchandise Mart. AE, D, DC, MC, V.
$$–$$$

OYSY The name of this Japanese bistro—pronounced oh-EE-she—means *delicious,* and that is the verdict of many diners who sample the *nigiri* (thin slices of raw fish on rice); the *maki* rolls (wrapped in dried seaweed); and the grilled and tempura dishes. The inexpensive lunch special—a $12 *bento* box filled with grilled fish or meat, maki, vegetable tempura, and tofu pancakes—is a favorite of Michigan Avenue office crowd. The place itself is sleek and modern, with translucent glass panels climbing lime and mustard walls, and seating in geometric blond-wood booths.
50 E Grand Ave, betw Rush and Wabash, 312/670-6750, oysysushi.com. El: Red to Grand. AE, D, DC, MC, V.
$$

● **PHIL STEFANI'S 437 RUSH** This Phil Stefani signature restaurant feels like a classic Italian steak house. The menu stars prime steaks, lobster tails, and pasta dishes as well as a *grigliata di pesce* (grilled swordfish, lobster, shrimp, and veggies) and an Australian lamb chop wrapped in *speck* (similar to prosciutto). Wine tastings take place every Friday at lunch (about $10 with your entrée).
437 N Rush St, betw Illinois and Hubbard, 312/222-0101, stefanirestaurants.com. No lunch Sat. Closed Sun. El: Red to Grand. AE, D, DC, MC, V.
$$$

● **PIZZERIA UNO** Chicago deep-dish pizza was born here in 1943. The slightly granular crust is heaped with meat, cheeses, and tomatoes, then baked in a deep-dish pan. The place was crowded out of the gate, spawning Pizzeria Due a decade later as well as Uno branches nationwide.
29 E Ohio St, at Wabash, 312/321-1000, pizzeriauno.com. El: Red to Grand. AE, D, DC, MC, V. Also: Pizzeria Due, 619 N Wabash Ave, betw Ohio and Ontario, 312/943-2400. El: Red to Grand.
$$

● **REDFISH** New Orleans–style cajun cooking is the focus here, and seafood dominates the menu. But if you don't feel like crab-stuffed salmon, coconut shrimp, or blackened catfish po'boys, you can always order hickory-smoked barbecue with pecan pie. Wednesday through Saturday there's live music, and Tuesday is karaoke night.
400 N State St, at Kinzie, 312/467-1600, redfishamerica.com. El: Red to Grand. AE, D, MC, V.
$$

WHERE MAGNIFICENT MILE AND STREETERVILLE

● **RIVA** Floor-to-ceiling windows with lake and skyline views dominate Navy Pier's sprawling top restaurant, which is decorated with model ships and other nautical paraphernalia. On the menu are steaks and seafood dishes such as salmon with wild rice and butternut-squash hash. There are two bars and a café with alfresco dining. 700 E Grand Ave, at Navy Pier, 312/644-7482, stefanirestaurants.com. Bus: 65 to Navy Pier. AE, D, DC, MC, V. $$$–$$$$

● **SHANGHAI TERRACE** A contemporary take on a 1930s Shanghai supper club, this intimate space in the Peninsula Hotel serves some of the city's best Chinese food. Lobster with Asian greens and yellow chives is a winner, as is the five-spice duck with stir-fried vegetables. It's definitely worth it for a special night. The terrace is lovely. 108 E Superior St, 4th fl, betw Michigan and Rush, 312/573-6744. Closed Sun. El: Red to Chicago. AE, D, DC, MC, V. $$$–$$$$

● **SHAW'S CRAB HOUSE** Shaw's is two restaurants in one: the main dining room, serving fish, sushi, and prime steaks; and the buzzy oyster bar, with a casual menu of oysters, popcorn shrimp, crab cakes, and live blues some days. 21 E Hubbard St, betw State and Wabash, 312/527-2722, shawscrabhouse.com. No lunch weekends. El: Red to Grand. AE, D, DC, MC, V. $$–$$$

● **SINGHA** Casual and affordable Singha is known for generous portions of Thai fare. Spring rolls, satay, *somtom* (papaya salad), and *tomka* (chicken-and-coconut-milk soup) stand out. 340 N Clark St, betw Kinzie and Chicago River, 312/467-0300. El: Brown, Purple to Merchandise Mart. AE, D, DC, MC, V. $$

● **676 RESTAURANT** Creative American fare like shrimp-and-corn chowder are draws at this Omni Chicago spot overlooking the Magnificent Mile. Bright chandeliers are overhead, and a hand-painted moonscape embellishes the ceiling.
676 N Michigan Ave, betw Huron and Erie, 4th floor, 312/944-7676. Also serves breakfast. El: Red to Chicago. AE, D, DC, MC, V.
$$–$$$

● **TRU** James Beard Award-winning chefs Rick Tramonto and Gale Gand offer stunningly progressive French cuisine in this chic, minimalist space hung with works by Warhol, Richter, and Ruscha. Caviar presented on a miniature glass staircase and lobster bisque served in a Versace espresso cup are noteworthy signature dishes.
676 N St Clair St, betw Huron and Erie, 312/202-0001, trurestaurant.com. No lunch; closed Sun. El: Red to Chicago. AE, D, DC, MC, V.
$$$$

● **VERMILION** Indian and Latin American cuisines meet on the menu of this popular after-work spot. In addition to traditional Indian dishes, chef Maneet Chauhan presents inventive tapas that pull from both cultures. Highlights: tandoori skirt steak, chili-glazed tamarind ribs, passion fruit-lemon tart. DJ Sergio spins exotic sounds between 6 and 11 on Friday.
10 W Hubbard St, betw Dearborn and State, 312/527-4060. No lunch weekends. El: Red to Grand. AE, D, DC, MC, V.
$$$

● **VTK** Superchef Jean-Georges Vongerichten goes Thai. Look for shrimp-and-crab pad thai; miso salmon; and, Tuesdays, whole Dungeness crab in chili sauce with tom yum soup and Thai beer—all for $35 a head. Family-style menus and outdoor tables, too.
6 W Hubbard St, betw State and Dearborn, 312/644-8664, vongsthaikitchen.com. No lunch Sun. El: Red to Grand. AE, D, MC, V.
$$–$$$

GOLD COAST AND OLD TOWN

Restaurants on Michigan Avenue are in this section if they're north of Chicago Avenue. Those to the south are in the Magnificent Mile and Streeterville section.

- 🟠 American
- 🔵 Chinese
- 🟠 European
- 🟠 Italian
- 🔵 Japanese
- 🔵 French and Contemporary
- 🔴 Latin
- 🟢 Mediterranean
- 🟤 Seafood
- 🔴 Steak
- 🟢 World

● **ASHKENAZ DELICATESSEN** Homemade potato pancakes, spinach knishes, noodle kugel, chopped liver, cheese blintzes, and overstuffed turkey and roast beef sandwiches are all on the menu at this Gold Coast deli.

12 E Cedar St, betw Lake Shore and State, 312/944-5006. Also serves breakfast. El: Red to Clark/Division. AE, MC, V.
$

● **BISTRO 110** Chef Dominique Tougne presides over this neighborhood favorite, popular for its traditional bistro cuisine. Try the Brie-stuffed baked artichoke; cassoulet with duck confit and garlic lamb sausage; the chicken Paul Bocuse (chicken fricassee with spinach and a cream sauce flavored with morels).

110 E Pearson St, betw Rush and Michigan, 312/266-3110, bistro110restaurant.com. Also serves brunch Sun. El: Red to Chicago. AE, D, DC, MC, V.
$$$

● **CAFÉ DES ARCHITECTES** The cuisine is contemporary French at this sleek restaurant in the Sofitel Water Tower. Pan-seared Maryland crab cake with roasted-sweet-pepper sauce is a favorite, along with herb-and-sun-dried-tomato risotto and roast chicken with crushed Peruvian potatoes. Priced at about $19, the lunchtime "30-minute meals" are a good deal if you want appetizer, salad, entrée, and diminutive dessert.

20 E Chestnut St, betw State and Wabash, 312/324-4063. Also serves breakfast daily and brunch weekends. El: Red to Chicago. AE, D, MC, V.
$$$

WHERE GOLD COAST AND OLD TOWN

● **CAPE COD ROOM** This landmark is a cozy nook in the formal Drake Hotel, with red-checkered tablecloths, low ceilings, and paneled walls festooned with mounted fish, seascapes, and nautical memorabilia. The experience is a good deal more formal than your standard Cape Cod beach shack, but

it's hard to fault the Dover sole, lobster tail, and oysters on the half shell. And the Bookbinder soup, spiked with sherry, is a local favorite.
140 E Walton Pl, at Michigan Ave at Walton St, 312/787-2200. El: Red to Chicago. AE, D, DC, MC, V.
$$$

● **CRU CAFÉ AND WINE BAR** Some 400 varieties of wine—including 50 by the glass—are available at this Gold Coast hangout, and the menu sets just the right notes to accompany them: oysters, salade Niçoise, lobster-and-beef-tenderloin club sandwich, cheese plates, caviar, pâté, and more. The kitchen stays open until just after midnight.

25 E Delaware St, betw Wabash and State, 312/337-4001, cruwinebar.com. El: Red to Chicago. AE, D, DC, MC, V. $$–$$$

● **DINOTTO RISTORANTE** Salmon with capers in a creamy, vodka-spiked tomato sauce and baked lasagna made with ground veal are representative selections on the menu this intimate Northern Italian in Old Town. There are daily specials, too.
215 W North Ave, betw Weiland and Wells, 312/202-0302, dinotto.com. No lunch Sun. El: Brown, Purple to Sedgwick. AE, D, DC, MC, V.
$$$

● **DITKA'S RESTAURANT** Legendary Bears coach Mike Ditka is the name behind this polished all-American just off the Magnificent Mile. Football memorabilia highlighting Ditka's career embellish the walls, and there's live music in the cigar lounge, where you'll find a large selection of premium cigars as well as cognacs and ports.
100 E Chestnut St, betw Rush and Michigan, 312/587-8989, mikeditkas chicago.com. Also serves brunch Sun; no lunch weekends. El: Red to Chicago. AE, D, DC, MC, V.
$$$

- **FIREPLACE INN** Barbecued ribs stand out at this Chicago favorite, but you can also order prime steaks and seafood. Some 24 TVs keep things lively. 1448 N Wells St, betw Schiller and Burton, 312/664-5264 (312/943-7427 for carryout or delivery), fireplaceinn.com. No lunch Mon–Thurs. El: Brown, Purple to Sedgwick. AE, D, MC, V. $$$

- **FOODLIFE** This is no ordinary food court: Instead of fries and pizza, look for Mexican and Asian fare, salads, pastas, grains, chicken, a light fare station, and more. Water Tower Place, Mezzanine Level, 835 N Michigan Ave, betw Chestnut and Pearson, 312/335-3663. El: Red to Chicago. AE, D, DC, MC, V. $

- **GIBSONS STEAKHOUSE** The steaks are prime and so is the people-watching at this buzzing Gold Coaster. Singles check each other out in the bar; power players hold forth in the packed dining room. Servers are unfazed. 1028 N Rush St, Oak and Bellevue, 312/266-8999, gibsonssteakhouse.com. El: Red to Chicago. AE, D, DC, MC, V. $$$

- **HUGO'S FROG BAR & FISH HOUSE** This bustling spot wins with plates of Maryland crab cakes and steaks from nearby Gibsons Steakhouse, among other pleasures. The bar opens at 3 pm and there's piano music nightly. 1024 N Rush St, at Bellevue, 312/640-0999, hugosfrogbar.com. El: Red to Chicago. AE, D, DC, MC, V. $$$

- **KAMEHACHI** Visiting celebrities who need a sushi fix beeline to this local sushi star. The kitchen scores, too, with tempura, teriyaki, and noodles. 1400 N Wells St, at Schiller, 312/664-3663, kamehachi.com. No lunch Sun. El: Brown, Purple to Sedgwick. AE, D, DC, MC, V. Also: 240 E Ontario St, betw Fairbanks and St Clair, River North, 312/587-0600. El: Red to Grand. 320 N Dearborn St, Westin River North Hotel, River North, 312/744-1900. El: Brown, Purple to Merchandise Mart. $$$

LE COLONIAL Shutters and palms recall Indochina in this vintage row house restaurant. Notable fare includes include sautéed shrimp and asparagus with a chili- and garlic-zapped satay sauce, and filet mignon with yams and string beans. There's outdoor seating. 937 N Rush St, at Walton, 312/255-0088, lecolonialchicago.com. El: Red to Chicago. AE, DC, MC, V.
$$$

NOMI Glass artist Dale Chihuly's stunning "Lumière d'Ambre" undulates along a wall of this seventh-floor Park Hyatt restaurant. Add great lake views and you'd have a can't-miss destination even without the lively menu by Christophe David. In warm weather, you can have your pan-roasted Maine lobster with curry emulsion alfresco. 800 N Michigan Ave, Chicago and Michigan, 312/239-4030, nomi restaurant.com. Also serves breakfast daily and brunch weekends. El: Red to Chicago. AE, D, DC, MC, V.
$$$$

PALM COURT High ceilings, fountains, plush couches, and antique paintings make an elegant backdrop for tea and cocktails in this Drake Hotel lounge. A harpist, pianist, and jazz quartet take turns. Some 20 brews are poured during afternoon tea time; after 5, the bar offers 100 wines with jazz or piano, plus dancing on weekends. 140 E Walton Pl, at Michigan, 312/932-4619. No lunch or dinner. El: Red to Chicago. AE, D, DC, MC, V.
$$

SALPICÓN At this modern Mexican on a quiet stretch of Wells, you can sample a flight of single-village mescals: Some 100 tequilas are on offer. The light, flavorful cuisine is from chef-owner Priscila Satkoff, and the room is vivid, with black-and-white-checked floors, fuschia linens, deep yellow walls, and bright Mexican art. The open-air café is lovely. 1252 N Wells St, betw Goethe and Scott, 312/988-7811, salpicon.com. Also serves brunch Sun; no lunch. El: Brown, Purple to Sedgwick. AE, D, DC, MC, V.
$$$

SIGNATURE ROOM AT THE 95TH For Chicagoans, this dressy John Hancock aerie is a special-occasion must, with dramatic views and contemporary cuisine—think slow-roasted lamb with goat-cheese polenta cake, and grouper with sun-dried tomatoes. Three-course dinners are a steal at $40. 875 N Michigan Ave, betw Chestnut and Delaware, 312/787-9596, signatureroom.com. Also serves brunch Sun; no lunch Sun. El: Red to Chicago. AE, D, DC, MC, V.
$$$

- **SPIAGGIA** This Italian, twice nominated for a James Beard Award, gives you an eyeful of Lake Michigan along with the cuisine of chef Missy Robbins. Many signature dishes are roasted in wood-fired ovens, and the seared scallops and guinea hen wrapped in pancetta are notable. A sister café, part of the restaurant complex, has a marvelous lake view and vivid murals. 980 N Michigan Ave, at Oak, 312/280-2750, spiaggiarestaurant.com. No lunch. El: Red to Chicago. AE, D, DC, MC, V.
$$$$

- **SPOON** At this trendy Old Towner, a long bar, leather banquettes, and a high-tech sound system set the scene for fun martinis and comfort food—grilled cheese, burgers, skirt steak. 1240 N Wells St, at Scott, 312/642-5522, spoonchicago.com. No lunch; closed Mon and Tues. El: Red to Clark/Division. AE, D, DC, MC, V.
$$

- **TAVERN ON RUSH** Here, chef John Gatsos pleases one and all with prime steaks and chops, fresh fish, pasta, daily specials, and a sprawling bar. 1031 N Rush St, at Bellevue, 312/664-9600, tavernonrush.com. Also serves breakfast Fri–Sun and brunch weekends. El: Red to Clark/Division. AE, D, DC, MC, V.
$$$

- **TWIN ANCHORS** Time warp prevails at this quaint, woody Old Town tavern with an eclectic jukebox and a vintage sign ordering POSITIVELY NO DANCING. Fans swear the ribs are worth the

wait; you can also order burgers, fish fry, or chili. Set on a residential Old Town street, the place appeared in the 2000 film *Return to Me*. 1655 N Sedgwick St, betw Eugenie and Concord, 312/266-1616, twinanchorsribs.com. No lunch weekdays. El: Brown, Purple to Sedgwick. AE, D, DC, MC, V.
$$–$$$

36　　　**WHERE TO EAT** WHEREVER YOU ARE

RIVER NORTH

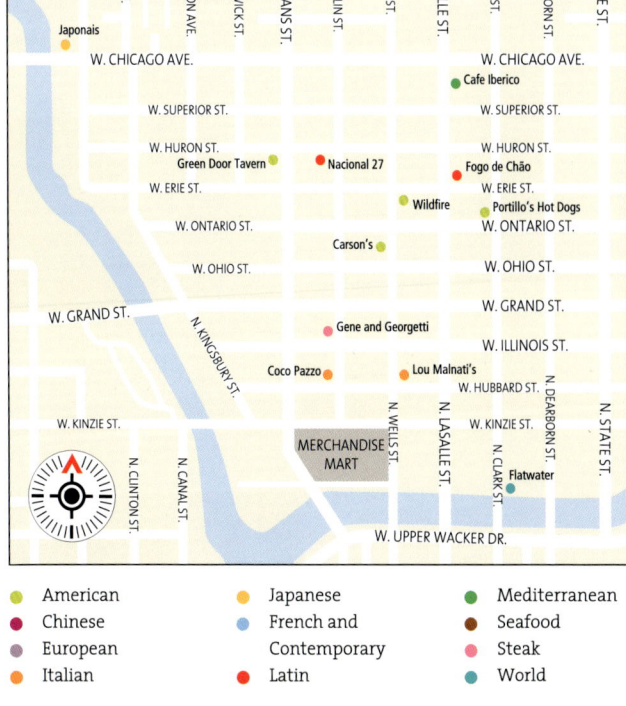

American

Chinese

European

Italian

Japanese

French and
Contemporary

Latin

Mediterranean

Seafood

Steak

World

● **CAFÉ IBERICO** A lively, cosmopolitan crowd of local Spaniards and tapas lovers packs this authentic, wide-open joint for pitchers of fruity sangria and tasty hot and cold small plates of marinated olives, grilled mushrooms with garlic, and baked goat cheese with tomato-basil sauce.
739 N LaSalle St, betw Chicago and Superior, 312/573-1510, cafeiberico.com. El: Red to Chicago. AE, D, MC, V.
$

● **CARSON'S** This Chicago classic has been dishing up sweet-sauced ribs, chicken, and pork chops since 1976. Michael Jordan, Janet Jackson, and Mayor Richard Daley have all come to pay homage.
612 N Wells St, betw Ontario and Ohio, 312/280-9200, ribs.com. El: Brown, Purple to Chicago. AE, D, MC, V.
$$–$$$

● **COCO PAZZO** Chef-partner Tony Priolo's outstanding regional cuisine makes this restaurant in a contemporary loft space one of the best Italians in town. The daily risotto specials are tempting, but don't miss the herb-crusted lamb with artichokes, peas, leeks, and fried potatoes, and pastry chef Erika Masuda's gelati and sorbets—from fresh mint and coconut-basil to prickly pear and pomegranate. Jackets are suggested for men.

300 W Hubbard St, at Franklin, 312/836-0900, cocopazzochicago.com. No lunch weekends. El: Brown, Purple to Merchandise Mart. AE, D, DC, MC, V.
$$$

● **FLATWATER** Sweet city views and an expansive menu of "global comfort food" draw after-work crowds to the lush water-level patio at this restaurant on the Chicago River. The menu includes everything from empanadas, Thai chicken wraps, and coconut-cashew curry to flatbreads with toppings like shellfish or tandoori chicken and tasting flights of hot dogs and beers. About 400 feet of front docking space make the place convenient for local boaters, and they stop by regularly to pick up meals to go.
321 N Clark St, River Level, off Kinzie, 312/644-0283, flatwater.us. Also serves breakfast. El: Brown, Purple to Merchandise Mart. AE, D, DC, MC, V.
$–$$

FOGO DE CHÃO Come hungry to this all-you-can-eat Brazilian meatery. Beef, lamb, pork, and more are carved tableside, and served with cheese bread, potatoes, polenta, and fried bananas. Even the salad bar is huge 661 N LaSalle St, at Erie, 312/932-9330, fogodechao.com. No lunch weekends. El: Brown, Purple to Chicago. AE, D, DC, MC, V.
$$$

GENE AND GEORGETTI Local power brokers hang out in this steak joint founded in 1941. Known for crusty, perfectly cooked USDA prime aged steaks, it also serves chops, seafood, and Italian dishes like chicken Vesuvio and veal limone. A fireplace cozies things up in winter.
500 N Franklin St, at Illinois, 312/527-3718, geneandgeorgetti.com. Closed Sun. El: Brown, Purple to Merchandise Mart. AE, D, DC, MC, V.
$$$

GREEN DOOR TAVERN Serving up hearty burgers and chili since 1921, the fireplace-warmed space, a former speakeasy, is comfortably cluttered with vintage political buttons, old signs, and other antique ephemera. 678 N Orleans St, betw Erie and Huron, 312/664-5496. El: Brown, Purple to Merchandise Mart. AE, D, MC, V.
$

JAPONAIS A stylish crowd and a menu of contemporary Japanese cuisine make this place a local hot spot. Every plate is exquisitely presented, from baked oysters with shrimp and bacon gratin to teriyaki-glazed tempura lobster with shiitake-rice stuffing. 600 W Chicago Ave, at Larrabee, 312/822-9600, japonaischicago.com. No lunch weekends. Bus: 66 to Larrabee. AE, MC, V.
$$$–$$$$

KIKI'S BISTRO On a quiet street lined with industrial buildings, this woody nook pleases regulars with bistro classics—roast quail and red cabbage on field greens, escargots with garlic butter, sautéed duck breast, apple tart. 900 N Franklin St, at Locust, 312/335-5454, kikisbistro.com. No lunch Sat; closed Sun. El: Brown, Purple to Chicago. AE, D, DC, MC, V.
$$$

- **LOU MALNATI'S** While not the city's biggest name in pizza, the pies may be its best, with their flaky, buttery crust and sweet, tomatoey sauce. Service is fast, and the memorabilia-decked, brick-walled, space is very kid-friendly. 439 N Wells St, at Hubbard, 312/828-9800, loumalnatis.com. El: Brown, Purple to Merchandise Mart. AE, D, DC, MC, V. $$

- **NACIONAL 27** Chef Randy Zweiban's buzzing Latino eatery explores the cuisine of two dozen nations. Try the plantain and boniato croquettes, the adobo-glazed pork tenderloin, spicy shrimp ceviche, or mango-sauced barbecued salmon. The bar pours mojitos and Brazilian caipirinhas. On Friday and Saturday, salsa plays until the early morning hours. 325 W Huron St, betw Orleans and Franklin, 312/664-2727, nacional27.net. No lunch; closed Sun. El: Brown, Purple to Chicago. AE, D, DC, MC, V. $$$

- **PORTILLO'S HOT DOGS** At this jumbo diner, shaved Italian beef comes piled atop French bread and soaked in its juice. Or you can go for Polish hot dogs, burgers, pasta, or salads. With more than 30 branches nationwide, the place is huge, with vintage signs, checkered tablecloths, and an antique car suspended from the ceiling, recalling 1920s through 1940s America. 100 W Ontario St, at Clark, 312/587-8910, portillos.com. El: Red to Grand. D, MC, V. $

- **WILDFIRE** All the meat dishes at this casual, cozy favorite are roasted on spits over an open fire. Look for prime rib, mushroom-crusted pork shop and horseradish-crusted filet, with mashed redskin potatoes on the side and peanut butter tart and apple pie. for dessert Try for a booth. 159 W Erie St, betw Wells and La Salle, 312/787-9000, wildfirerestaurant.com. El: Brown, Purple to Chicago. AE, D, DC, MC, V. $$$

LOOP

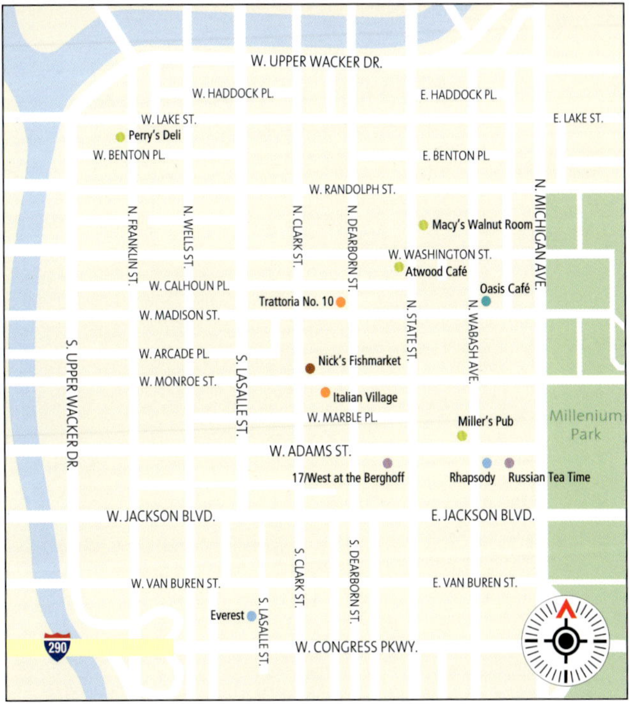

Restaurants

- Everest
- Rhapsody
- Russian Tea Time
- 17West at the Berghoff
- Miller's Pub
- Italian Village
- Nick's Fishmarket
- Trattoria No. 10
- Oasis Café
- Atwood Café
- Macy's Walnut Room
- Perry's Deli

Legend

- 🟢 American
- 🟣 Chinese
- 🟪 European
- 🔴 Italian
- 🟡 Japanese
- 🔵 French and Contemporary
- 🔴 Latin
- 🟢 Mediterranean
- 🟤 Seafood
- 🩷 Steak
- 🩵 World

WHERE TO EAT WHEREVER YOU ARE

● **ATWOOD CAFÉ** Red velvet brackets the immense windows at this high-ceilinged restaurant in a turn-of-the-20th-century building, where American fare gets a creative twist. Start with duck quesadillas or tuna-and-salmon tartare, then go for rosemary-crusted pork tenderloin or,

for lunch, the chicken potpie.
1 W Washington St, at State, 312/368-1900, atwoodcafe.com. Also serves breakfast. El: Red to Lake. AE, D, DC, MC, V.
$$–$$$

● **EVEREST** The food lives up to the view in this many-chandeliered, white-and-gold room on the 40th floor of the Chicago Stock Exchange. Chef-owner Jean Joho's cuisine is a contemporary take on the culinary traditions of his native Alsace—think black cod with pumpernickel-horseradish crust or roast lobster in Gewürztraminer-ginger butter sauce. The several multicourse prix fixe options showcase the talent in the kitchen, and every plate is exquisite; one risotto is topped with gold leaf.
1 Financial Pl, 440 S LaSalle St, 40th fl, betw Van Buren and Congress Pkwy, 312/663-8920, everestrestaurant.com. No lunch; closed Sun and Mon. El: Loop to LaSalle. AE, D, DC, MC, V.
$$$$

● **ITALIAN VILLAGE** Chicago's oldest Italian restaurant, opened in 1927, today includes three restaurants: contemporary Vivere, the casual Village, and steak-and-seafood La Cantina, with booth seating and jumbo fish tanks as entertainment. The wine list is the Midwest's largest, a *Wine Spectator* Grand Award recipient every year since 1984.
71 W Monroe St, betw Clark and Dearborn, 312/332-7005, italianvillage chicago.com. El: Red, Blue to Monroe. AE, D, DC, MC, V.
$$–$$$

MACY'S WALNUT ROOM Marshall Field's may now be Macy's, but the landmark store's restaurant continues to charm with its country-club feel and fine city views. The lunch menu includes all the favorites—quiche, meatloaf, chicken potpie. During holidays, locals love to dine under the huge Christmas tree. 111 N State St, 7th fl, betw Washington and Randolph, 312/781-3125. No dinner. El: Red to Lake. AE, D, DC, MC, V. $$–$$$

MILLER'S PUB Established in 1935, this American restaurant with leatherette booths and formica-topped tables is famous for its baby-back ribs but also

does great steaks, chops, and chicken. The kitchen stays open until 2 am and the bar until 4. Look for vintage photos of TV and radio celebs like Milton Berle and George Burns on the walls. 134 S Wabash Ave, betw Adams and Monroe, 312/263-4988, millerspub.com. El: Loop to Quincy. AE, D, DC, MC, V. $$

NICK'S FISHMARKET & GRILL Since the late 1970s, this airy restaurant has been a favorite after-work spot. Grilled fish comes with a Parmesan crust or with citrus-ginger, Asian barbecue, or lemon-butter sauces; mixed seafood grills and solid meat options round out the menu. The grill area aims for a younger professional crowd, with five champagnes by the glass, spacious booth seating, and a casual menu. 51 S Clark St, betw Monroe and Madison, 312/621-0200, nicksfishmarket chicago.com. No lunch Sat; closed Sun. El: Blue to Monroe. AE, D, MC, V. $$$$

OASIS CAFÉ The Middle Eastern food is among the city's best, despite the modest setting. Lentil soup, falafel sandwiches, and hummus star. 17 S Wabash Ave, betw Madison and Monroe, 312/443-9534. El: Brown, Green, Orange, Purple to Madison. AE, D, DC, MC, V. $

- **PERRY'S DELI** The line snakes out the door for gargantuan sandwiches here. Call out your order and watch the turkey, corned beef, and salami pile up. But remember: It's cash only, and cell phones are strictly forbidden.
180 N Franklin St, betw Couch and Lake, 312/372-7557, perrysdeli.com. Also serves breakfast; no dinner; closed weekends. El: Loop to Washington. No credit cards.
$

- **RHAPSODY** The sophistication of the American cuisine at this Symphony Center spot makes the experience as delicious as it is convenient. The cured yellowfin tuna starter, with blood orange emulsion, Peking duck gnocchi with hibiscus flowers, and seared walleye with fiddleheads and pink-grapefruit butter keep mealtime interesting. Expect preconcert crowds.
65 E Adams St, betw Wabash and Michigan, 312/786-9911, rhapsody chicago.com. No lunch weekends. El: Red to Jackson. AE, D, DC, MC, V.
$$–$$$

- **RUSSIAN TEA TIME** During afternoon teas, this Art Institute-area restaurant offers many brews—plus gorgeous scones with Devon cream, lemon curd, savories, and sweets. At mealtime, go for the classic latkes, blinis, borschts.
77 E Adams St, betw Michigan and Wabash, 312/360-0000, russianteatime.com. El: Loop to Adams. AE, D, MC, V.
$$$

- **17/WEST AT THE BERGHOFF** Known for its German food and creaky waiters, the Berghoff has new ownership and a new menu that adds contemporary choices like sliced steak with polenta to its classic schnitzels and sauerbratens. But the dark oak trim and vintage murals appear blessedly unchanged..
17 W Adams St, at State, 312/427-3170, 17westchicago.com. El: Red, Blue to Monroe. AE, MC, V.
$$

- **TRATTORIA NO. 10** This pretty Theater District Italian serves excellent fresh fish, handmade ravioli, and other classics with contemporary flair.
10 N Dearborn St, betw Dearborn and Calhoun, 312/984-1718, trattoriaten.com. No lunch Sat; closed Sun. El: Loop to Monroe. AE, D, DC, MC, V.
$$$

44   **WHERE TO EAT** WHEREVER YOU ARE

RANDOLPH MARKET AND RIVER WEST

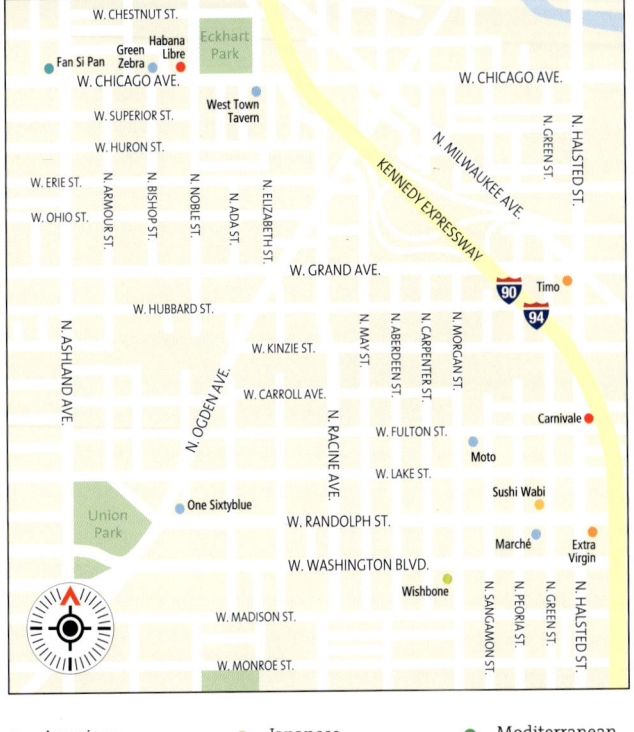

- American
- Chinese
- European
- Italian
- Japanese
- French and Contemporary
- Latin
- Mediterranean
- Seafood
- Steak
- World

- **CARNIVALE** In this behemoth, heavy velvet drapes, jumbo light fixtures, and supersaturated colors set the scene for fun South American nibbles such as empanadas, scallop ceviche, chimichurri-topped skirt steak, and rum-glazed pork shoulder. Don't miss the weekend specials.

702 W Fulton Market, at Union, 312/850-5005, carnivalechicago.com. No lunch weekends. El: Pink, Green to Clinton. AE, D, DC, MC, V.
$$–$$$

- **EXTRA VIRGIN** At this wine bar, the menu offers small plates—antipasti, bruschetta, savory seared sea scallops with beets and goat cheese, figs with prosciutto and mozzarella. Black-and-white photography and mellow green Tuscan tiles make the space soothing. 741 W Randolph St, at Halsted, 312/474-0700. No lunch Sat; closed Sun. Bus: 8 to Randolph. AE, D, MC, V.
$$$

- **FAN SI PAN** Here, Vietnamese spring rolls come with fillings like chicken with kaffir lime, lemongrass, ginger, mint, and basil—along with sides like curried sweet potatoes with coconut-milk gravy and green-papaya salad. 1618 W Chicago Ave, betw Ashland and Marshfield, 312/738-1405. Closed Sun. Bus: 66 to Ashland. D, MC, V.
$

- **GREEN ZEBRA** James Beard Award-winning chef Shawn McClain takes vegetarian cuisine to new heights at this lovely, Zen-like spot. The menu might include roasted-beet-and-blue-cheese ravioli, parsnip *panna cotta*, eggs with smoked potato puree, or sweet potato dumplings with water chestnuts and dandelion miso broth. You'll usually find a couple of fish dishes and one organic poultry as well. 1460 W Chicago Ave, at Greenview, 312/243-7100, greenzebrachicago.com. No lunch. Bus: 66 to Ashland. AE, D, DC, MC, V.
$$$

HABANA LIBRE Classic Cuban specialties like ham croquettes and black bean soup welcome you to this modest West Town storefront. The lunch special—say, a Cubano sandwich with ham, pork, and Swiss cheese—is a steal at $5.99. BYOB.
1440 W Chicago Ave, at Bishop, 312/243-3303. Bus: 66 to Bishop. MC, V.
$–$$

MARCHÉ The paintings are eclectic and the colors bold at this theatrical restaurant, a celebration of the European brasserie. Classics such as escargots and steak *frites* are on the menu, along with contemporary takes on Provençal fare.
833 W Randolph St, at Green, 312/226-8399, marche-chicago.com. No lunch. Bus: 8 to Randolph. AE, D, DC, MC, V.
$$$

MOTO Young chef Homaro Cantu, who spent four years at Charlie Trotter's, has food lovers all over town studying his technology-powered, conceptual "postmodern cuisine." Liquid helium and nitrogen, a centrifuge, an ion particle gun, and a laser are all pressed into service to manipulate exquisite ingredients from local and global sources to create astonishing fare: lobster with orange soda, freeze-dried pina colada and doughnut soup. Sommelier Matthew Gundlach's small-batch vintages pair perfectly with the food. Bring a wide-open mind.
945 W Fulton Market Ave, betw Morgan and Sangamon, 312/491-0058, motorestaurant.com. No lunch; closed Sun and Mon. Bus: 20 to Morgan. AE, D, MC, V.
$$$$

- **ONE SIXTYBLUE** In designer Adam Tihany's stylish room, butter yellow mixes with cobalt, and chef Martial Noguier takes a playful approach to American-French cooking. Look for arctic char with glazed fennel and lobster-licorice sauce; baby coho salmon on wild-rice blini.
1400 W Randolph St, at Ogden, 312/850-0303, onesixtyblue.com. No lunch; closed Sun. El: Green, Pink to Ashland. AE, MC, V.
$$$

- **SUSHI WABI** A black-clad crowd, live DJs, and a creative menu of *nigiri* and *maki* keep this place hip. Try the tarantula roll, a mouthful of soft-shell crab, fresh crab, cucumber, avocado, and chili sauce.
842 W Randolph St, betw Peoria and Green, 312/563-1224, sushiwabi.com. No lunch weekends. Bus: 8 to Randolph. AE, D, DC, MC, V.
$$$

- **TIMO** Here, chef John Bubala offers a menu of wood-fire-roasted meats such as rabbit with applewood bacon and handmade *pappardelle* and braised lamb shanks. The patio is a fabulous alfresco dining spot.
464 N Halsted St, betw Hubbard and Grand, 312/226-4300, thymechicago.com. No lunch; closed Mon. El: Blue to Grand. AE, MC, V.
$$$

- **WEST TOWN TAVERN** Contemporary comfort food is the order of the day at this relaxed bistro; herb-roasted wild-mushroom flatbread with truffle oil, and duck confit with mashed parsnips and caramelized shallots stand out.
1329 W Chicago Ave, at Throop, 312/666-6175, westtowntavern.com. No lunch; closed Sun. Bus: 66 to Greenview. AE, MC, V.
$$–$$$

- **WISHBONE** Platters here come heaped with black-eyed peas and jambalaya, while surreal chickens and whimsical art entertain Chicagoans of all stripes.
1001 W Washington Blvd, at Morgan, 312/850-2663, wishbonechicago.com. Also weekday breakfast and weekend brunch; no dinner Sun-Mon. Bus: 20 to Morgan. 3300 N Lincoln, at Marshfield, Lakeview, 773/549 4105. Bus: 11 to School. AE, D, DC, MC, V.
$$

WHERE TO EAT WHEREVER YOU ARE

GREEKTOWN AND WEST LOOP

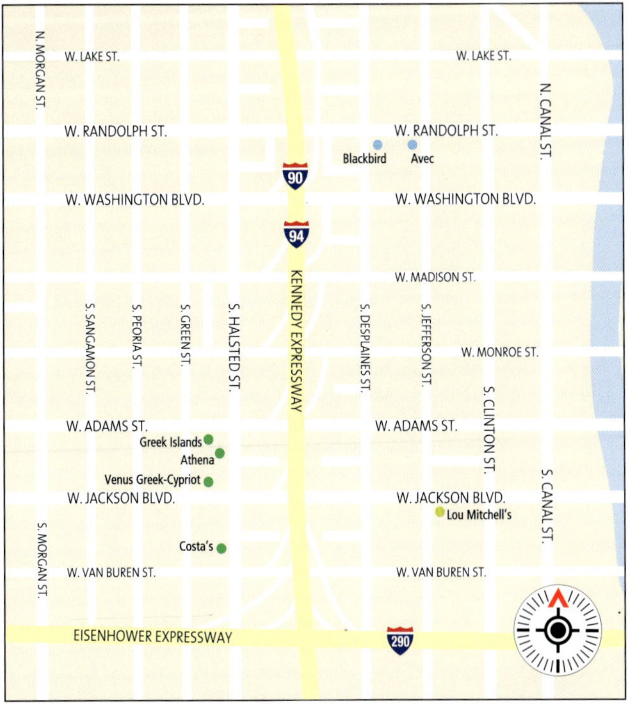

N. MORGAN ST.

W. LAKE ST.

W. LAKE ST.

N. CANAL ST.

W. RANDOLPH ST.

W. RANDOLPH ST.

90

Blackbird   Avec

W. WASHINGTON BLVD.

W. WASHINGTON BLVD.

94

W. MADISON ST.

S. SANGAMON ST.

S. PEORIA ST.

S. GREEN ST.

S. HALSTED ST.

KENNEDY EXPRESSWAY

S. DESPLAINES ST.

S. JEFFERSON ST.

W. MONROE ST.

S. CLINTON ST.

S. CANAL ST.

W. ADAMS ST.

W. ADAMS ST.

Greek Islands

Athena

Venus Greek-Cypriot

W. JACKSON BLVD.

W. JACKSON BLVD.

Lou Mitchell's

S. MORGAN ST.

Costa's

W. VAN BUREN ST.

W. VAN BUREN ST.

EISENHOWER EXPRESSWAY

290

- American
- Chinese
- European
- Italian
- Japanese
- French and Contemporary
- Latin
- Mediterranean
- Seafood
- Steak
- World

● **ATHENA** At this Greek bistro from restaurateur Pete Tsoukalas, you'll find traditional Greek dishes like spanakopita and souvlaki, plus grilled fresh seafood and vegetables.
212 S Halsted St, betw Jackson and Adams, 312/655-0000. El: Blue to UIC-Halsted. AE, DC, MC, V.
$$

● **AVEC** A sophisticated crowd makes its way to this corporate sibling of perennial hot spot Blackbird, next door, for the smart wine selection and a menu that offers wood-fired pizzas, housemade pastas, a cheese selection, and rustic small plates (chorizo-stuffed dates, hangar steak, curry-spiked skate with cilantro and lime). The room is modern and minimalist; the cedar walls and ceiling, stainless steel bar, and rear glass wall full of wine bottles make the narrow space feel almost spa-like. Good people-watching keeps ennui from setting in as you wait for a table at the bar.
615 W Randolph St, betw Jefferson and Desplaines, 312/377-2002, avec restaurant.com. No reservations. El: Green, Pink to Clinton. AE, D, DC, MC, V.
$$$

BLACKBIRD James Beard Award-winning chef Paul Kahan is at the helm of this contemporary American restaurant known for its complex, sophisticated seasonal cuisine. Kahan's menu includes dishes like braised octopus with hummus, charred ramps, sesame brittle, and chickpeas; pan-roasted monkfish with Parmesan, prosciutto, ruby grapefruit, and salsify; and sautéed organic veal sweetbreads with braised baby romaine, country ham, fresh shell beans, and truffles. The space is sleek and busy, with an outdoor space that's pleasant when the weather's warm.
619 W Randolph St, betw Jefferson and Desplaines, 312/715-0708, blackbird restaurant.com. No lunch Sat; closed Sun. El: Green, Pink to Clinton. AE, D, DC, MC, V.
$$$

COSTA'S One of Greektown's fanciest restaurants, this white-tablecloth spot is all about seafood. Shrimp Costa's comes sautéed with spinach, garlic, lemon, and pine nuts and served on angel hair pasta—it's excellent. You can also order Greek dishes like moussaka and gyros.
340 S Halsted St, betw Van Buren and Jackson, 312/263-9700. El: Blue to UIC-Halsted. AE, D, DC, MC, V.
$$–$$$

GREEK ISLANDS This restaurant bustles at lunch and dinner daily with business types and other locals tucking into gyros, lamb with artichokes, grilled octopus, and other Greek specialty. The family-style dinner is a steal at $19.95 per person.
200 S Halsted St, at Adams, 312/782-9855. El: Blue to UIC-Halsted. AE, D, DC, MC, V.
$$–$$$

- **LOU MITCHELL'S** This old-school diner near Union Station feels as if it has been around forever, and that's practically true—it has been serving fluffy

omelets, pancakes, and other morning favorites since 1923; it's such a classic, in fact, that it even has its own article on Wikipedia. Whenever you go, you will probably have to wait, and it's then that you will experience one of the quirks that has made the place so lovable: Without explanation, they hand you little boxes of Milk Duds (at lunch) or doughnut holes (at breakfast). Nobody seems to mind that the most recent remodeling is practically ancient history or that the place doesn't accept credit cards—in any case, there's an ATM on the premises. 565 W Jackson Blvd, betw Jefferson and Clinton, 312/939-3111. Also serves breakfast; no dinner. El: Brown, Purple, Orange to Quincy. No credit cards. $

- **VENUS GREEK-CYPRIOT CUISINE** More than 100 different traditional Greek and Cypriot dishes are on the menu at this Greektown spot, including lamb meatballs, pork tenderloin, and the delectable signature *kleftiko* (lamb wrapped in foil, baked for six hours, and served with roasted potatoes). The bar here is shaped like an ancient Mediterranean warship, complete with mast and draped flags. There's traditional music Friday and Saturday from 9 pm until 2 am. 820 W Jackson Blvd, betw Green and Halsted, 312/714-1001, venuschicago.com. No lunch Mon–Sat. El: Blue to UIC-Halsted. AE, D, DC, MC, V. $–$$

52   **WHERE TO EAT** WHEREVER YOU ARE

SOUTH LOOP AND CHINATOWN

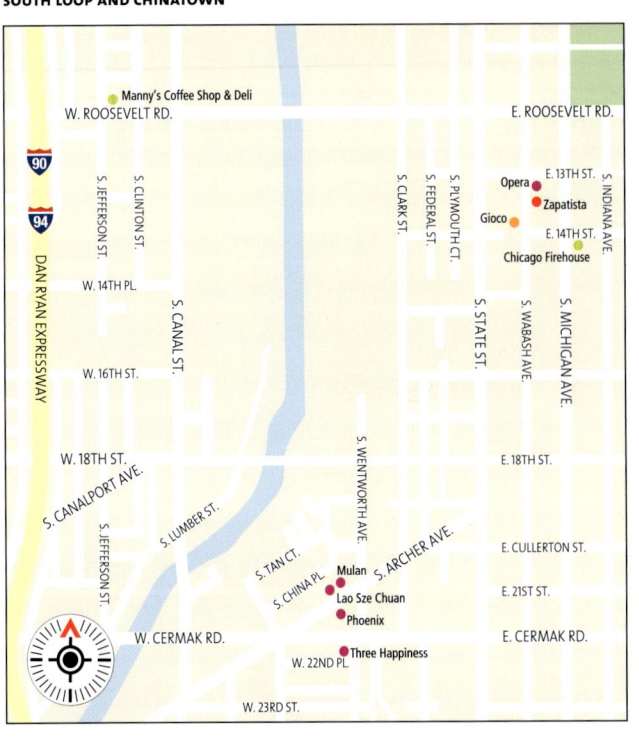

- 🟡 American
- 🔴 Chinese
- 🟣 European
- 🟠 Italian
- 🟡 Japanese
- 🔵 French and Contemporary
- 🔴 Latin
- 🟢 Mediterranean
- 🟤 Seafood
- 🟣 Steak
- 🔵 World

● **CHICAGO FIREHOUSE RESTAURANT** This restored fire station is a handsome setting for classic American fare — steaks, seafood, and salads, plus sandwiches at lunch. Seating is in the bar, a dining room, and a wine cellar. 1401 S Michigan Ave, at 14th, 312/786-1401, chicagofirehouse.com. No lunch weekends. El: Red to Roosevelt. AE, D, MC, V.
$$–$$$

● **GIOCO** Housed in an 1890s building, Gioco suggests a Prohibition-era speakeasy, stylishly updated. The menu lists regional Italian dishes with a contemporary twist—pork chops stuffed with fontina cheese, grapes, and sage, with Swiss chard and apple cider reduction on the side. Prime steaks, pastas, and thin-crust pizza from a wood-fired oven round things out. 1312 S Wabash Ave, betw 13th and 14th, 312/939-3870, gioco-chicago.com. Also serves brunch Sun; no lunch weekends. El: Red to Roosevelt. AE, D, DC, MC, V.
$$$

● **LAO SZE CHUAN** This Chinatown favorite focuses on the cuisine of southwest China. Dishes such as pea-pod chicken, beef with oyster sauce, Peking duck, and moo shu vegetables are easy to love; more challenging for western palates are traditional options such as jellyfish Shanghai style and stir-fried kidneys. The kitchen stays open until midnight.

2172 S Archer Ave, Chinatown Square strip mall, betw Cermak and Wentworth, 312/326-5040, laoszechuan.com. El: Red to Cermak Chinatown. AE, D, MC, V.
$$

MANNY'S COFFEE SHOP & DELI

Chicago's best corned beef is one of the draws of this South Loop cafeteria established in 1942. The breakfast and lunch fare—from omelets and French toast to mile-high deli sandwiches—is outstanding, appreciated by a motley crew of cops, old-timers, and UIC students.
1141 S Jefferson St, betw Taylor and Roosevelt, 312/939-2855. Also serves breakfast; no dinner; closed Sun. Bus: 12 to Jefferson. Also: Midway Airport. Also serves breakfast. El: Orange to Midway. AE, D, MC, V.
$

MULAN

In this stunning minimalist space with an open kitchen, suede benches, and glowing light columns, chef-designer Kee Chan (creator of Old Town's Heat restaurant) serves Asian-fusion seafood plates. Try the tuna sashimi with blood-orange marinade and quail egg; pork with green mussel pâté; duck breast with dried seahorse and ginger risotto; or Australian beef tenderloin with spiny-lobster mashed potatoes.
2017 S Wells St, Chinatown Square strip mall, betw Cermak and Wentworth, Level 2, 312/842-8282, mulanrestaurant .com. El: Red to Cermak-Chinatown. AE, D, MC, V.
$$$–$$$$

OPERA

Executive chef Paul Wildermuth is the power behind the contemporary Chinese menu at this gorgeous South Loop style-setter. Jewel-hue reds, blues, and greens make the setting wild and flamboyant; the frenetic open kitchen and a giant oil painting that slides back to reveal a private dining room are equally riveting. On the menu, look for Maine lobster spring rolls with mango lime dressing, three-course Peking duck, and slow-roasted Scottish salmon with smoked salmon and chives and caramelized tangerine sauce. The house special whole red

snapper is steamed with bamboo, ginger, scallions, mushrooms, and wine, then doused with roasted sesame oil—delicious. There's a good vegan selection, and on Tuesdays, $25 buys you any starter or salad, plus an entrée and dessert.
1301 S Wabash Ave, at 13th, 312/461-0161, opera-chicago.com. No lunch. El: Red to Roosevelt. AE, D, DC, MC, V.
$$$

● **PHOENIX RESTAURANT** Hong Kong-style Cantonese dishes make up the menu at this popular giant in the heart of Chinatown. Live fish and lobsters are prepared to order, or go for two-course Peking duck. The chef's special lobster sauce is a house favorite, and there's dim sum through lunchtime—though if you don't arrive early, you'll wait more than you probably care to.
2131 S Archer Ave, 2nd fl, Cermak and Wentworth, 312/328-0848. Also serves breakfast. El: Red to Cermak-Chinatown. AE, D, MC, V.
$$–$$$

● **THREE HAPPINESS RESTAURANT** If you want dim sum in Chicago, this is the spot. After lunchtime, look for good Cantonese and Szechuan cuisine. Carryout and delivery are available, and the kitchen stays open virtually around the clock. One of the city's top Chinese restaurants. Note that the New Three Happiness restaurant nearby is a completely different place.
209 W Cermak Rd (opposite Chinatown Fire Station), at Wentworth, 312/842-1964 or 312/842-1970. Also serves breakfast. El: Red to Cermak-Chinatown. AE, D, MC, V.
$

● **ZAPATISTA** Rustic wood tables, traditional Mexican tiles, and bright orange, green, and yellow walls set a festive mood here. Chef Dudley Nieto creates authentic Mexican fare ranging from seared shrimp in *guajillo-morita* salsa to grilled chicken breast with tamarind-chipotle glaze and crab cakes with red and yellow peppers and mole verde. Guacamole is prepared tableside, tortillas are made fresh on premises, and fajitas are served on a lava stone. The bar pours many tequilas as well as blended specialty drinks. The huge, shady outdoor café can be idyllic.
1307 S Wabash Ave, betw 13th and 14th, 312/435-1307, zapatistacantina.com. El: Red to Roosevelt. AE, D, DC, MC, V.
$$

56 **WHERE TO EAT** WHEREVER YOU ARE

PILSEN AND LITTLE ITALY

● American	● Japanese	● Mediterranean
● Chinese	● French and	● Seafood
● European	Contemporary	● Steak
● Italian	● Latin	● World

🟠 **AL'S #1 ITALIAN BEEF** Founded in 1938, Al's #1 Italian Beef can now be found all over the metro area, but only this original location has Little Italy style. The thinly sliced beef is served on French bread, dry or dipped, with sweet peppers and *giardiniera* (sliced vegetables). There's no table seating: Lean on the counter rails or chow down out in your car. For dessert, there's Mario's Italian Lemonade across the street.
1079 W Taylor St, betw Aberdeen and Carpenter, 312/226-4017, alscatering.com. El: Blue to Racine. No credit cards. $

🔴 **BOMBON** The Pilsen neighborhood is Chicago's epicenter of Mexican culture, and this European-style pastry shop owned by Luis Perea and Laura Cid-Pfeiffer, formerly of Frontera Grill/Topolobampo, shows a Mexican side in its sandwiches and in confections like its margarita and white-chocolate-and-mango cakes. A Gold Coast location, BomBon Americano, sells whimsical, colorful American-style cupcakes and fruit tarts.
1508 W 18th St, betw Laflin and Ashland, 312/733-7788, bomboncafe.com. Also serves breakfast. El: Blue to 18th. AE, D, MC, V. Also: BomBon Americano, 1000 N Clark St, at Oak, Gold Coast, 312/787-7717. Bus: 22 to Oak. $

🔴 **CUERNAVACA** At this long-established family-owned spot, you can expect Mexican standbys like burritos, tacos, and fajitas along with house specials like *pescado y camarones* (fish and shrimp) and *pollo asado* (roast chicken). Lush plants, colorful decorations, and a jukebox stocked with Mexican favorites make the place lively and welcoming.
1160 W 18th St, betw May and Racine, 312/829-1147. No lunch. El: Blue, Pink to 18th. AE, D, DC, MC, V. $

● **MAY STREET CAFÉ** Appearing like an oasis on an industrial stretch of Cermak Road is this restaurant serving seasonal takes on Mexican, Cuban, Puerto Rican, and American dishes. Imaginatively prepared quesadillas and tortillas open for lamb, pork, and steak entrées. The candlelight draws out the deep reds and blues of the intimate dining room. BYOB. 1146 W Cermak Rd, at May, 312/421-4442, maystcafe.com. No lunch; closed Mon. El: Red to Cermak-Chinatown. Bus: 21 to May. AE, MC, V.
$$

● **MUNDIAL-COCINA MESTIZA** A trio of Chicago restaurant veterans teamed up to open this bright terra-cotta-and-ceramic-tile-clad Pilsen store-front. The eclectic menu highlights Mexican and Mediterranean cuisine, from *tortas* and *panini* and crepes at lunchtime to ceviche, shrimp dishes, and rib eye for dinner. The children's menu lists kid-friendly staples such as burgers and chicken nuggets. BYOB. 1640 W 18th St, betw Marshfield and Paulina, 312/491-9908. Also serves breakfast. El: Blue, Pink to 18th. AE, D, MC, V.
$

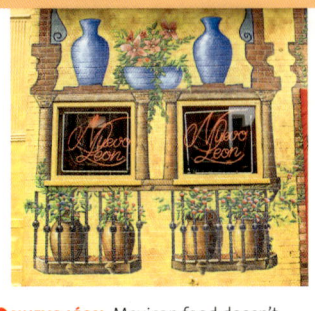

● **NUEVO LÉON** Mexican food doesn't get any more authentic than at this cheerful Mexican diner founded in 1962; look for huevos rancheros, fajitas, tacos, enchiladas, and specialty plates with chicken, steak, and tongue. BYOB. 1515 W 18th St, betw Laflin and Ashland, 312/421-1517, nuevoleon restaurant.com. Also serves breakfast. El: Blue to 18th. No credit cards.
$

● **SKYLARK** In this classic tavern, antique Masonic lodge banners and a portrait of early-20th-century-mayor Anton Cermak provide the décor, and the kitchen does a good job with burgers, vegetarian chili, and mac and cheese. The crispy tater tots have cult status among regulars. A fish fry every Friday, and there's a great beer selection. 2149 S Halsted St, at Cermak, 312/948-5275. No lunch. El: Blue to Halsted. Bus: 8 to Cermak. No credit cards.
$

● **TUFANO'S VERNON PARK TAP** Established in 1930, this casual eatery has served home-style southern Italian fare in Little Italy. The lemon chicken and high-piled lightly breaded calamari earn raves, but you'll also find eggplant Parmesan, pork chops, and pasta with broccoli, mushrooms, marinara sauce, and such. 1073 W Vernon Park Pl, betw Carpenter and Aberdeen, 312/733-3393. No lunch weekends; closed Mon. El: Blue to Racine. No reservations. No credit cards. $$

● **TUSCANY** This large, lively Little Italy hot spot is popular for its homemade pastas and its meats, seafood, and pizzas cooked over wood fires; grilled octopus, roast chicken, and Dover sole with lobster cream sauce hold pride of place on the menu. The restaurant looks contemporary enough with its green-check tablecloths and open kitchen, but the servers' white shirts and black slacks and the older, well-dressed crowd make the place feel like a bit of old Chicago. 1014 W Taylor St, betw Miller and Morgan, 312/829-1990. No lunch weekends. El: Blue to Racine. AE, D, DC, MC, V. Also: 3700 N Clark St, at W Waveland, Lakeview, 773/404-7700. El: Red to Addison.
$$–$$$

WHERE TO EAT WHEREVER YOU ARE

BUCKTOWN AND WICKER PARK

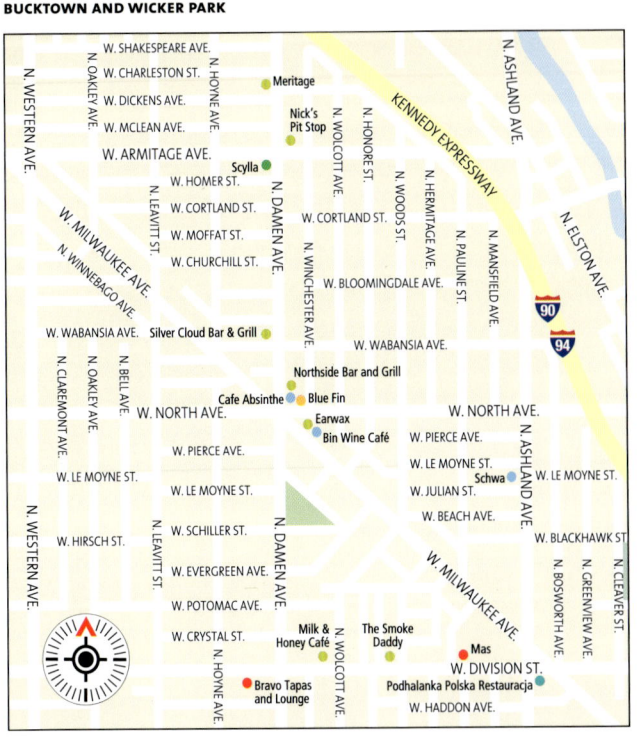

● **BIN WINE CAFÉ** At this relaxed neighborhood hangout, 36 wines come by the glass (and 75 by the bottle) to go with the food: thin-crust pizzas cooked in a wood-burning oven; interesting starters like house-cured duck prosciutto and skate tartine; and hearty entrées like coq au vin and spring English pea and mint ravioli with lamb ragout. There's a good selection of cheeses, and your munching options include several different cheese flights.
1559 N Milwaukee Ave, south of W North Ave, 773/486-2233, binwinecafe.com. Also serves brunch weekends; no lunch. El: Blue to Damen. AE, D, DC, MC, V.
$$

● **BLUE FIN** In this stylish, candlelit sushi spot in buzzing Wicker Park, sushi rolls include lobster hand rolls, the "Chicago" with salmon and eel, and the "Ronin," with two kinds of tuna, yellowtail, red snapper, and Scottish salmon. But it's not all sushi: Scallops come grilled with sweet rice and coconut sauce, and the tuna steak is cooked, albeit served very rare. 1952 W North Ave, betw Damen and Winchester, 773/394-7373, bluefinsushibar.com. El: Blue to Damen. AE, D, DC, MC, V.
$$–$$$

BRAVO TAPAS AND LOUNGE Classics like pan-seared shrimp with white-wine-and-garlic sauce, bacon-wrapped dates stuffed with chorizo, and a sea-food ceviche in creamy garlic-chipotle sauce draw crowds to this hot tri-level tapas spot. A 26-foot waterfall dominates the bold interior, which is all reds, mustards, and metallic blues and browns. An open-air mojito bar does a brisk business Thursday, Friday, and Saturday (when there's also disco in a cool, candlelit downstairs lounge), and there's live Latin music Tuesday and Friday and a live flamenco show every other Sunday.
2047 W Division St, betw Hoyne and Damen, 773/278-2727. Bus: 70 to Damen. AE, MC, V.
$–$$

CAFÉ ABSINTHE Wicker Park couples coo over sophisticated, French-inspired fare at this longtime neighborhood favorite, established in 1994. Chefs in the buzzing open kitchen whip up plates of herb-marinated lamb with garlic gratin and crispy duck breast with confit ravioli. You enter through an alley just north of the restaurant.
1954 W North Ave, betw Damen and Winchester, 773/278-4488. No lunch. El: Blue to Damen. AE, D, DC, MC, V.
$$$

EARWAX At this colorful veteran of the Wicker Park alternative scene, vegans and carnivores alike go for the reasonably priced fare—from veggie and beef burgers to breakfast food and Mexican specialties. You can browse the selection of books and magazines for sale before grabbing a table under one of the enormous antique circus canvases hanging from the walls. An ATM is on the premises.
1561 N Milwaukee Ave, betw North and Honore, 773/772-4019, earwaxcafe.com. Also serves breakfast. El: Blue to North. No credit cards.
$

● **MAS** Chef John Manion whips up reliably good Nuevo Latino fare at this Wicker Park hot spot. Top picks include chile-braised chicken tostada with refried black beans; spiced fried shrimp with arepas and salsa; chili-cured pork tenderloin with white beans and truffle-scented jus; and New York strip steak with chipotle mash. The margaritas are killer, and they're just $5 on Mondays (along with mojitos and martinis); bottles of wine are half price on Tuesday; and on Wednesday, a tasting menu paired with wine goes for $45. There's outdoor dining.
1670 W Division St, at Paulina, 773/276-8700, masrestaurant.com. No lunch. El: Blue to Division. AE, MC, V.
$$$

● **MERITAGE** Chef Troy Graves keeps regulars smiling at this intimate long-time favorite with bold, global fare: caramelized onion and blue cheese tart with huckleberry coulis, Maryland crab cake with tangerine and chili emulsion; snail and black truffle ravioli, served with parsnip bisque; and pork chops with ginger-rhubarb chutney and goat-cheese mashed potatoes. The patio and deck are lovely.
2118 N Damen Ave, at Charleston, 773/235-6434, meritagecafe.com. Also serves brunch Sun; no lunch. Bus: 50 to Armitage. AE, D, DC, MC, V.
$$–$$$

● **MILK & HONEY CAFÉ** This charmer serves homemade breakfast pastries and granola, plus sandwiches and good specials.
1920 W Division St, betw Wolcott and Winchester, 773/395-9434. No dinner. Bus: 70 to Damen. AE, D, DC, MC, V.
$$

● **NICK'S PIT STOP** For roast chicken, this is the place: a counter-service dive whose grill is lined with row after row of roasting birds. A few bucks gets you a quarter light or dark; the chicken pita sandwich is a steal at $4.25.
2011 N Damen Ave, betw Armitage and McLean, 773/342-9736. Closed Sun. Bus: 50 to Armitage. MC, V.
$

WHERE BUCKTOWN AND WICKER PARK

● **NORTHSIDE BAR AND GRILL** Perfect for people-watching, this hip eatery has a large greenhouse-atrium dining area that opens onto a patio. The chefs turn out American cuisine with international notes: sandwiches, salads, burgers, and seafood preparations. 1635 N Damen Ave, betw Milwaukee and Concord, 773/384-3555, northsidechicago.com. El: Blue to Damen. AE, D, MC, V.

$$

● **PODHALANKA POLKSA RESTAURACJA**

Chicago is home to the largest concentration of Poles outside Warsaw, and for a taste of authentic Polish fare without a trek to the city's outlying neighborhoods, you can't do better than this no-frills former tavern on a strip in Wicker Park once known as "Polish Broadway" because of all the Polish bars that used to be here. Borscht, homemade pierogi, potato pancakes, and pork rolls are among the restaurant's filling and inexpensive dishes. 1549 W Division St, betw Ashland and Bosworth, 773/486-6655. Also serves breakfast. El: Blue to Division. AE, D, MC, V.

$

● **SCHWA** A tiny hidden gem on a sparse stretch of Ashland in Wicker Park, this restaurant highlights organic cuisine from buzzed-about chef Michael Carlson. In his minuscule open kitchen, Carlson relies on sustainable ingredients for such dishes as boneless quail with chorizo and *judion* (Spanish butter beans) and the vegan roast made with peanuts, potatoes, soy, and basil. You can order either a four- or nine-course menu; either way, ask what will be on the menu when you arrive so that you can bring the proper wine. And whatever you do, reserve well in advance, as the few tables go quickly. 1466 N Ashland Ave, at Le Moyne, 773/252-1466, schwarestaurant.com. No lunch; closed Sun and Mon. BYOB. El: Blue to Division. MC, V.

$$

- **SCYLLA** Creative, Mediterranean-inspired seafood plates star in this cozy Bucktown space from chef-owner Stephanie Izard. Look for grilled baby octopus with prosciutto, ramps, fava beans, and preserved lemon; skate wing and pork belly with rhubarb compote; and sautéed gnocchi with Manila clams, white asparagus, green garlic, and truffle-poblano broth.
1952 N Damen Ave, betw Homer and Armitage, 773/227-2995, scyllarestaurant.com. No lunch; closed Mon. Bus: 50 to Armitage. AE, D, DC, MC, V. $$

- **SILVER CLOUD BAR & GRILL** As far as Chicago diners go, this retro Bucktown spot is one of the best. Expect nicely executed American fare—burgers, meat loaf, chicken potpie, pot roast. Check out the list of microbrews and martinis, and note that cigars are welcome after 10 pm.
1700 N Damen Ave, at Wabansia, 773/489-6212, silvercloudchicago.com. Also serves brunch weekends. El: Blue to Damen. AE, D, DC, MC, V. $$

- **THE SMOKE DADDY** Live blues and jazz and platters of pulled pork and slow-smoked brisket, ribs, and chicken, with sweet potato fries on the side, draw Wicker Park meat lovers to this low-key retro-meets-industrial space. The veggie barbecue sandwich is also good. Sides of macaroni and cheese and collard greens, plus pecan and key lime pies, round out the menu.
1804 W Division St, betw Wood and Honore, 773/772-6656, thesmokedaddy.com. El: Blue to Division. AE, D, DC, MC, V. $–$$

WHERE TO EAT WHEREVER YOU ARE

LINCOLN PARK

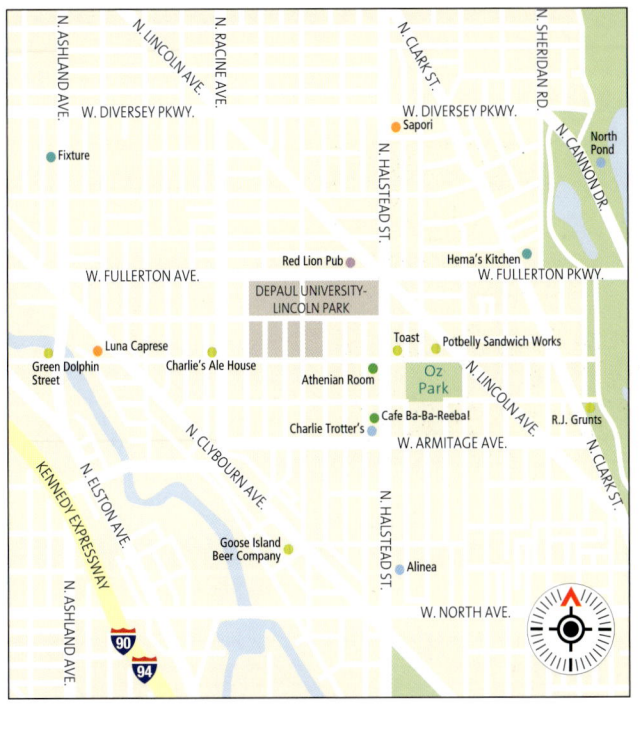

Legend:
- American
- Chinese
- European
- Italian
- Japanese
- French and Contemporary
- Latin
- Mediterranean
- Seafood
- Steak
- World

- **ALINEA** Culinary star Grant Achatz is one of a handful of American chefs practicing so-called molecular gastronomy, with its experiments in edible physics and chemistry, and his first solo venture is this minimalist space in Lincoln Park The menu changes daily. But whether you go for the 12-course tasting ($135) or the 24-course tour ($195), you can expect some wild stuff on the way, and it's all as fascinating and delicious as it is unusual. Bison with cranberry, persimmon, and juniper aroma, anyone?
1723 N Halsted St, betw North and Willow, 312/867-0110, alinea-restaurant.com. No lunch; closed Mon and Tues. El: Red to North/Clybourn. AE, D, DC, MC, V.
$$$$

- **ATHENIAN ROOM** Cheap Greek-style eats are the draw at this classic, casual Lincoln Park spot, which serves big plates of gyros, kebabs, burgers, pita sandwiches, and Greek salads. The signature kalamata half-chicken is baked in lemon-wine sauce, then broiled until the skin is crispy. No alcohol is served, but you can buy drinks at the adjacent Glascott's Groggery, and bring them to your table.
807 W Webster Ave, at Halsted, 773/348-5155. El: Blue to UIC-Halsted. MC, V.
$

● **CAFÉ BA-BA-REEBA!** Lincoln Park's top tapas spot scores with its buzz, its breezy patio, and its roster of reliably good small plates like citrus-cured salmon on cucumber bread, meatballs with sherry-tomato sauce, and *toro brochetas*—skewers of shrimp, chicken, pork, or beef paired with different sauces.
2024 N Halsted St, betw Armitage and Dickens, 773/935-5000, cafebabareeba .com. No lunch weekdays. Bus: 8 to Armitage. AE, D, MC, V.
$–$$

● **CHARLIE'S ALE HOUSE** A relaxed atmosphere, great beer selection, and a comfort-food menu—think chili, pot roast, and chicken potpie—make this local hangout a comfortable option for a quick bite. There are three locations around town.
1224 W Webster Ave, at Magnolia, 773/871-1440, charliesalehouse.com. Also serves brunch Sun; no lunch Wed and Thurs. El: Brown, Purple to Armitage. AE, D, DC, MC, V. Also: 700 E Grand Ave, at Navy Pier, Streeterville, 312/595-1440. Bus: 65 to Navy Pier. 5308 N Clark St, at Berwyn, Andersonville, 773/751-0140. Bus: 22 to Berwyn.
$$

● **CHARLIE TROTTER'S** Much-lauded chef-owner Charlie Trotter almost single-handedly led the meat-loving City of the Big Shoulders into the world of contemporary cooking and in the process earned a national reputation for his progressive approach, his complex cuisine. He relies on a network of suppliers for ultrafresh ingredients and with his vegetable juice-based vinaigrettes, light stocks, and delicate broths, he proves that food doesn't have to be rich to be sublime. Prix-fixe options include the eight-course meal ($145) and a vegetable dégustation ($125). A jacket for men and reservations are required.
816 W Armitage Ave, betw Dayton and Halsted, 773/248-6228, charlietrotters .com. No lunch; closed Sun and Mon. El: Brown, Purple to Armitage. AE, D, DC, MC, V.
$$$$

- **FIXTURE** Small plates are oh-so-stylish at this Lincoln Park spot from the owners of Bucktown's beloved Meritage. The menu includes Korean barbecued short ribs with kimchi and scallion emulsion, roasted suckling pig with barbecue-and-pineapple marmalade, crab-and-asparagus-stuffed artichoke, and peppered elk carpaccio with goat cheese and chestnut honey.
2706 N Ashland Ave, betw Wrightwood and Diversey, 773/248-3331, fixturechicago.com. No lunch. Bus: 9 to Diversey, 76 to Ashland. D, DC, MC, V.
$–$$

- **GOOSE ISLAND BEER CO.** Chicago's oldest brewpub was founded back when craft brewing was a novelty, particularly in the Midwest, and it's still going strong with two locations—in Lincoln Park and Wrigleyville. There are 10 handcrafted brews on tap every day, along with a menu of steaks, fresh seafood, salads. The signature Stilton burger is delicious. Brewery tours take place every Sunday at 3 ($3).
1800 N Clybourn Ave, at Willow, 312/915-0071, gooseisland.com. El: Red to North/Clybourn. AE, D, DC, MC, V. Also: 3535 N Clark St, betw Eddy and Cornelia, 773/832-9040. El: Red to Addison
$$

- **GREEN DOLPHIN STREET** Photos of jazz musicians deck the walls of this 1940s-style dining spot. The menu is all about meat; look for whitefish in lemon-butter-caper sauce, dry-aged Porterhouse, or lamb chops, with sides of chopped salad, spinach salad, mashed sweet potatoes, or truffled macaroni and cheese. Every night there's live jazz in the adjoining concert room.
2200 N Ashland Ave, at Webster, 773/395-0066, jazzitup.com. No lunch; closed Mon. Bus: 9 to Webster. AE, D, MC, V.
$$$

- **HEMA'S KITCHEN** Chef-owner Hema Potla cooks what many describe as the best Indian food in the city. Try the tikka masala, marinated in yogurt, lemon, and spices, or other specialties from southern India. BYOB.
2411 N Clark St, betw Fullerton and Arlington, 773/529-1705. Bus: 22, 36 to Fullerton. AE, MC, V. Also: 6406 N Oakley Ave, at Devon, Rogers Park, 773/338-1627. BYOB. Bus: 155 to Rockwell. AE, D, DC, MC, V.
$$ s

● **LUNA CAPRESE** The cuisine of Campania is on show at this cozy trattoria from Capri native Pietro Cristillo, with a mural of the Blue Grotto in back. The handmade pastas are subtly, simply sauced; the marinara is lovely. The *saltimbocca alla Romana* (veal with prosciutto and sage), chicken *Sorrentino* (with marinara sauce, eggplant, and mozzarella), and chicken *al limone* stand out. 2239 N Clybourn, near Greenview, 773/281-4825, lunacaprese.com. Bus: 74 to Greenview. AE, D, MC, V. $–$$

● **NORTH POND** The stunning Lincoln Park setting is a smart Prairie-style former ice skaters' shelter with a fieldstone fireplace and nine-foot French doors with the city skyline as a backdrop. In the kitchen is James Beard Award nominee Bruce Sherman, whose stints in France and India are reflected in his cuisine—asparagus velouté soup with minted goat cheese dumpling, black bass filet with crab-coconut-mango sambar, cinnamon-spiced duck with parsnip pancakes. 2610 N Cannon Dr, Fullerton and Diversey, 773/477-5845, northpond restaurant.com. Also serves brunch Sun; serves lunch June–Sept, Tues–Fri only; closed Mon. Bus: 151 to Wrightwood. AE, D, DC, MC, V. $$$–$$$$

● **POTBELLY SANDWICH WORKS** Baked sandwiches are on the menu at this folksy, friendly branch of an Illinois chain that started out as an antiques store. Try the Wreck: salami, roast beef, turkey, and ham with Swiss cheese. 2264 N Lincoln Ave, betw Webster and Belden, 773/528-1405. Bus: 11 to Webster. Also: 508 N Clark St, betw Illinois and Grand, River North, 312/644-9131. El: Red to Grand. 190 N State St, betw Benton and Lake, Loop, 312/683-1234. El: Red, Green, Orange, Pink, Brown to State/Lake. potbelly.com AE, D, MC, V. $

- **RED LION PUB** British memorabilia adorns every wall, and there's a real London telephone booth in the dining area. Order a bitter, a snakebite, or a black and tan—they're perfect with fish-and-chips or a ploughman's lunch (here, salad with bread and fruit). 2446 N Lincoln Ave, betw Fullerton and Montana, 773/348-2695. Bus: 11 to Fullerton. AE, MC, V.
$$

- **R.J. GRUNTS** The first of many eateries in the booming Lettuce Entertain You empire, Grunts is famous for its salad bar, blue cheeseburgers, and super-thick milkshakes. 2056 N Lincoln Park W, betw Dickens and Armitage, 773/929-5363, leye.com. Bus: 22, 36 to Armitage. AE, D, MC, V.
$$

- **SAPORI** This bustling trattoria is a neighborhood favorite thanks to friendly service—diners are often greeted with hearty handshakes or hugs—and generous portions of well-executed Italian food. The spaghetti *Barese,* thick noodles with veal meatballs and Italian sausage in marinara sauce, is possibly the best in town. *Cappellacci,* pasta stuffed with pumpkin or lobster, is a good bet, too, as are the risottos and gnocchi. 2701 N Halsted St, at Schubert, 773/832-9999. No lunch. Bus: 8 to Schubert. AE, D, DC, MC, V.
$$

- **TOAST** Mascarpone-stuffed French toast, blueberry buckwheat pancakes, and egg dishes like crabby eggs Benedict and spinach-and-goat-cheese omelets are the draw of this breakfast favorite. The lunch menu offers good sandwiches like turkey and Brie with honey mustard, and seared ahi tuna with mango chutney. 746 W Webster St, betw Burling and Halsted, 773/935-5600. Also serves breakfast; no dinner. Bus: 8 to Webster. AE, D, DC, MC, V. Also: 2046 N Damen Ave, betw McLean and Dickens, Bucktown/Wicker Park, 773/772-5600. Bus: 50 to Armitage.
$

WHERE TO EAT WHEREVER YOU ARE

LAKEVIEW

American
Chinese
European
Italian

Japanese
French and Contemporary
Latin

Mediterranean
Seafood
Steak
World

- **ADESSO** Here, the dining room's minimalist style puts the focus squarely on the regional Italian cuisine. Crisp *arancini* (rice balls) open for gnocchi dressed with butter, Parmesan, and caramelized squash. The *tagliata* (sliced steak on arugula) and the short ribs with polenta rate among entrées.

Don't miss the burger—topped with arugula pesto and provolone and served with rosemary-perfumed fries. Weekends, come early, while the music's low.
3332 N Broadway St at Aldine, 773/868-1516, eatadesso.com. BYOB. Bus: 36 to Buckingham. AE, D, MC, V. $

- **ANN SATHER** The gooey cinnamon buns are legendary at this classic, which was started by a small-town girl who liked to bake in 1945. The menu reflects her Scandinavian origins but mixes old favorites like Swedish pancakes with burgers, salads, and wraps; some of the recipes remain Ann Sather originals.
929 W Belmont Ave, at Wilton, 773/348-2378, annsather.com. Also serves breakfast; no lunch Tues; no dinner. El: Red, Brown, Purple to Belmont. AE, MC, V. Also: 3416 N Southport Ave, betw Roscoe and Newport, 773/404-4475. El: Brown to Southport. AE, DC, MC, V. 3411 N Broadway St, betw Hawthorne and Roscoe, Lakeview, 773/305-0024. Bus: 36 to Roscoe. AE, DC, MC, V. 5207 N Clark St, at Foster, Andersonville, 773/271-6677. Bus: 22 to Foster. AE, DC, MC, V.
$–$$

- **BITTERSWEET** Mouthwatering cakes, pies, tarts, brownies, cookies, and other confections fill the brightly lighted cases at this airy, charming bakery, but you can also order coffee or sandwiches to consume at one of the tables scattered around the room. Neighborhood residents love the place, but its fame has spread, so it is often busy and crowded.
1114 W Belmont Ave, betw Clifton and Seminary, 773/929-1100. Also serves breakfast; no dinner Mon. El: Red, Brown, Purple to Belmont. MC, V.
$

CHICAGO DINER The global vegan and vegetarian fare at this natural restaurant attracts locals and celebs. Look for lentil-and-tempeh shepherd's pie, lasagna with tofu ricotta, and a Reuben made with seitan. 3411 N Halsted St, betw Roscoe and Newport, 773/935-6696, veggiediner .com. El: Red, Brown, Purple to Belmont. AE, D, DC, MC, V.
$$

COOBAH In this spirited Latin restaurant, the food of Cuba, Colombia, Brazil, and the Philippines fuel the menu—think Caesar salad with sugarcane dressing, calamari with lime zest and parsley, steak with tarragon chimichurri. The Southport Avenue location is convenient late at night, and there's a DJ. 3423 N Southport Ave, betw Roscoe and Newport, 773/528-2220, coobah .com. Also serves brunch weekends; no dinner Mon in summer. El: Brown to Southport. AE, D, DC, MC, V.
$$$

D'AGOSTINO'S The pizza is addictive here—the crust crunchy, the sauce slightly sweet and lightly herbed. West of Wrigley Field. 1351 W Addison St, at Southport, 773/477-1822, dagostinospizza.com. El: Red to Addison. AE, D, MC, V.
$

DELEECE Offerings are eclectic and interesting at this unassuming spot: lobster-stuffed potato skins, salmon with black rice and pear-ginger sauce. 4004 N Southport Ave, at Irving Park Rd, 773/325-1710, deleece.com. Also serves brunch weekends; no lunch Mon. Bus: 80 to Southport. AE, D, MC, V.
$$$

DUKE OF PERTH Walking sticks and vintage bric-a-brac deck this relaxed pub with a robust offering of draft ales and single-malts scotches plus shepherd's pie and fish-and-chips. 2319 N Clark St, betw Surf and Oakdale, 773/477-1741, dukeofperth.com. No lunch Mon. Bus: 22 to Oakdale. AE, MC, V.
$

● **ERWIN** Chef Erwin Dreschler's innovative American menu pays homage to seasonal ingredients from around the Midwest. The arugula salad is made with with applewood-smoked bacon, pears, Gorgonzola, and maple-cider vinaigrette; the roast whitefish comes with rutabaga and spinach; the onion tart is spiked with blue cheese, walnuts, and sage.
2925 N Halsted St, betw George and Oakdale, 773/528-7200, erwincafe.com. Also serves brunch Sun; no lunch; closed Mon. Bus: 8 to Wellington. AE, D, DC, MC, V.
$$

● **404 WINE BAR** You sit on overstuffed couches at this inviting hangout with two fireplaces. But the real point is the varied wine pours and the bar menu of plates such as caramelized baked Brie and pear-walnut bruschetta.
2852 N Southport Ave, betw George and Wolfram, 773/404-5886. Bus: 76 to Southport. AE, D, DC, MC, V.
$$–$$$

● **HARMONY GRILL** Images of blues and country-and-western legends hang above copper-topped tables in this restaurant adjoining Schuba's, a popular music venue. The menu offers meat loaf, gumbo, and mac and cheese, plus a few global items. The kitchen relies on Midwest ingredients.
3159 N Southport Ave, at Belmont, 773/525-2528, schubas.com. El: Red, Brown to Belmont. AE, D, DC, MC, V.
$

● **INTELLIGENTSIA COFFEE** This local roaster has a simple mantra: source great green coffee, roast daily, serve extraordinary drinks. No wonder such restaurants as Charlie Trotter's and Alinea order from Intelligentsia.
3123 N Broadway St, betw Briar and Barry, 773/348-8058. Also serves breakfast. El: Red, Brown, Purple to Belmont. Also: 53–55 E Randolph St, betw Wabash and Garland, Loop, 312/920-9332. El: Loop to Randolph. 53 W Jackson Blvd, betw Federal and Dearborn, Loop, 312/253-0594. El: Red, Blue to Jackson. AE, D, MC, V.
$

JACK'S ON HALSTED
Blue Man Group is practically next door to this consistently good American restaurant at a busy intersection in the heart of Lakeview, so it's a pretheater favorite. The menu gives you options like strip steak, filet mignon with three-cheese twice-baked potato, and grilled lemongrass-crusted salmon with stir-fried rice; there's a separate menu for kids. Window tables give you a front-row seat on the lively street scene. 3201 N Halsted St, at Belmont, 773/244-9191, jackjonesrestaurants .com. Also serves brunch Sun; no lunch. El: Brown, Purple, Red to Belmont. AE, D, DC, MC, V. $$

JULIUS MEINL
Viennese coffeehouse traditions live on at this sole American outpost of the famed Austrian coffee purveyor. The light menu includes goulash, *käsespätzle* (tiny cheesy dumplings), crepes, and sandwiches, all served on a silver platter. The gorgeous cakes and tortes are best enjoyed with a good book and a leisurely cup of Meinl's own rich coffee. 3601 N Southport Ave, at Addison, 773/868-1857, meinl.com. El: Red to Addison, Brown to Southport. AE, D, DC, MC, V. $

KIT KAT LOUNGE AND SUPPER CLUB
Trendy food comes with cabaret at this restaurant with white leather sofas and stone-topped tables. Female impersonators portray Eartha Kitt, Marilyn Monroe, Carmen Miranda, and other celebs, while the whimsical menu roams from coconut shrimp to

ahi tuna. The martinis are fancy (and half-price on Sunday and Tuesday). You can have your meal al fresco on the patio when the weather's pleasant. 3700 N Halsted St, at Waveland, 773/525-1111, kitkatchicago.com. No lunch; closed Mon. El: Red to Addison. AE, D, DC, MC, V. $$$

- **LA TAVERNETTA** Friendly and family-run, this candlelit, subterranean spot makes all its lasagnas, gnocchis, and ravioli. If there's a wait, pop upstairs to Monsignor Murphy's bar. Allow time for parking—it can be a challenge here. 3023 N Broadway St, betw Barry and Wellington, 773/929-8787. No lunch. Bus: 36 to Barry. MC, V. $

- **MIA FRANCESCA** This place is always buzzing, and for regulars, the close-packed tables and the bustle are part of the draw, long with the lovely back garden. Rome's cuisine takes center stage; look for pasta, risotto, grilled fish, thin-crust pizzas. 3311 N Clark St, betw Buckingham and Aldine, 773/281-3310. No lunch weekdays. Bus: 22 to Aldine. Also: 1039 W Bryn Mawr St, Andersonville, 773/506-9261. El: Red to Bryn Mawr., miafrancesca.com. AE, D, DC, MC, V. $$

- **TANGO SUR** This Argentine grill is loud and dark, and a line forms nightly. Huge portions of meat and very reasonable prices explain the crowds—and most folks take home doggie bags 3763 N Southport Ave, at Grace, 773/477-5466. No lunch Sun. BYOB. Bus: 80 to Southport. AE, D, MC, V. $$

- **THAI CLASSIC** Baseball fans and regulars vie for pillowy raised platforms at this spacious restaurant known for its weekend buffets and friendly service. Spring rolls and crab wontons make good starters, and the shrimp pineapple curry, and pad thai are popular. 3332 N Clark St, betw Buckingham and Roscoe, 773/404-2000, thaiclassicrestaurant.com. BYOB. Bus: 22 to Newport. AE, D, DC, MC, V. $

- **YOSHI'S CAFÉ** Japanese, Italian, French, and American cuisines rendezvous at this storefront founded by fusion pioneer Yoshi Katsumura. One week, the inventive menu might star a crab-rich spring roll with edamame coulis; another might bring cajun-spiced skate. 3257 N Halsted St, betw Aldine and Melrose, 773/248-6160, yoshiscafe.com. Also serves brunch Sun; no lunch; closed Mon. El: Red, Brown, Purple to Belmont. AE, DC, MC, V. $$$

78 WHERE TO EAT WHEREVER YOU ARE

ROSCOE VILLAGE AND NORTH CENTER

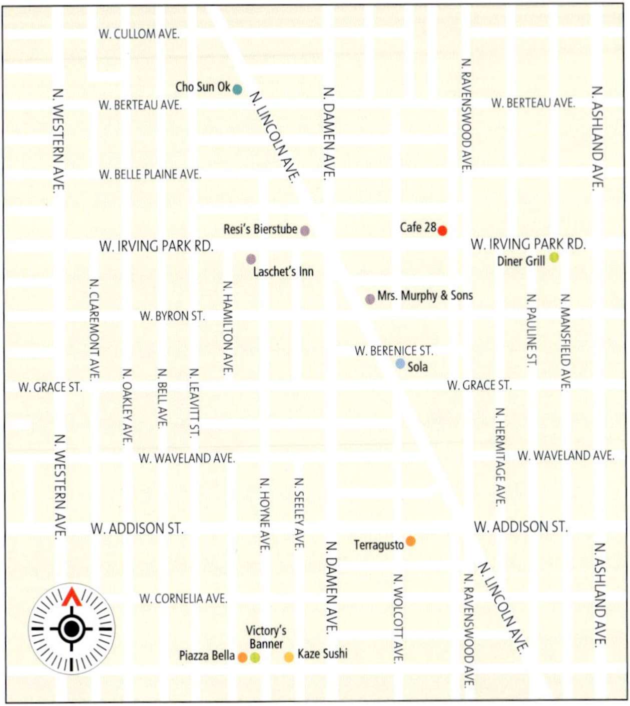

W. CULLOM AVE.

Cho Sun Ok

W. BERTEAU AVE.

N. WESTERN AVE.

N. LINCOLN AVE.

N. DAMEN AVE.

N. RAVENSWOOD AVE.

W. BERTEAU AVE.

N. ASHLAND AVE.

W. BELLE PLAINE AVE.

Resi's Bierstube

Cafe 28

W. IRVING PARK RD.

W. IRVING PARK RD.

Diner Grill

Laschet's Inn

Mrs. Murphy & Sons

N. CLAREMONT AVE.

W. BYRON ST.

N. HAMILTON AVE.

N. PAULINE ST.

N. MANSFIELD AVE.

W. BERENICE ST.

Sola

N. OAKLEY AVE.

N. BELL AVE.

N. LEAVITT ST.

W. GRACE ST.

W. GRACE ST.

N. HERMITAGE AVE.

W. WAVELAND AVE.

W. WAVELAND AVE.

N. WESTERN AVE.

N. HOYNE AVE.

N. SEELEY AVE.

W. ADDISON ST.

W. ADDISON ST.

Terragusto

N. DAMEN AVE.

N. WOLCOTT AVE.

N. LINCOLN AVE.

N. RAVENSWOOD AVE.

N. ASHLAND AVE.

W. CORNELIA AVE.

Victory's Banner

Piazza Bella

Kaze Sushi

American	Japanese	Mediterranean
Chinese	French and Contemporary	Seafood
European		Steak
Italian	Latin	World

● **CAFÉ 28** When the usual Cuban and Mexican staples appear on the menu at this cantina with exposed brick walls, there's always something a little special about it. The options are eclectic, ranging from Serrano-ham-wrapped asparagus and roast pork and caramelized onions on garlic polenta to marinated skirt steak with poblano rice, honey-jalapeño pork chops, and garlicky Cuban-style chicken. Sip on a mojito, the bar specialty, as you ponder the choices. 1800 W Irving Park Rd, at Ravenswood, 773/528-2883, cafe28.org. Also serves brunch weekends. El: Brown to Irving Park. AE, D, DC, MC, V.
$

● **CHO SUN OK** Chicago's oldest Korean restaurant looks a bit formidable from the outside since there are no windows, but frequent lines outside the door suggest the pleasures that await inside. There, small groups sit at a round table with a stone griddle, used for cooking seasoned meats such as *cha-dol gui* (thinly sliced beef)—the house specialty. The buckwheat noodles and various *panchan*, pickled vegetable dishes, are great sides. The place is tiny, so go early to avoid a wait. 4200 N Lincoln Ave, at Berteau, 773/549-5555, chosunokrestaurant.com. El: Brown to Irving Park. AE, D, MC, V.
$

● **DINER GRILL** After Chicago bars have closed, night owls with the munchies squint under unforgiving fluorescent lights and gobble down burgers and breakfast plates at this throwback to the '50s. Basically, it's a brick trailer with a long white counter, 12 stools, and no tables, and it has been serving meals around the clock since the days of countertop jukeboxes—which are still going strong here. 1635 W Irving Park Rd, at Marshfield, 773/248-2030. El: Brown to Irving Park. No credit cards.
$

KAZE SUSHI In this minimalist sushi spot, chef Macku Chan serves a progressive menu of miso-grilled alligator, sweet potato soup with lob-

ster broth, and deep-fried whitefish-wrapped shrimp served with parsley butter sauce. Black and green teas and asparagus show up in desserts. 2032 W Roscoe St, at Seeley, 773/327-4860, kazesushi.com. No lunch. Bus: 50 to Roscoe. AE, D, DC, MC, V. $$–$$$

LASCHET'S INN Cozy red-checkered-tablecloth Laschet's serves the same inexpensive, stick-to-your-ribs schnitzels and goulashes it did when it opened in 1971. *Spaetzle,* red cabbage, and roasted potatoes are the sides, and top German brews are on tap. 2119 W Irving Park Rd, between Hoyne and Hamilton, 773/478-7915, laschets inn.com. No lunch weekdays. El: Brown to Irving Park. AE, D, MC, V. $

MRS. MURPHY & SONS IRISH BISTRO In this lofty white-tablecloth room with a fireplace and its gorgeous hand-carved teak bar, the Irish dining revolution is evident—witness duck breast with vanilla-spiked demiglace and sautéed walleye with acorn squash and apple puree, and Guinness-zapped onion soup. 3905 N Lincoln Ave, at Byron, 773/248-3905, irishbistro.com. No lunch weekends; closed Mon. El: Brown to Irving Park. AE, D, MC, V. $$

PIAZZA BELLA TRATTORIA Classic Italian fare comes at fairly moderate prices here, especially chicken dishes, pastas, pizzas, and lunchtime Italian sandwiches. The wine list includes more than 80 wines, half Italian. 2116 W Roscoe St, betw Hamilton and Hoyne, 773/477-7330, piazzabella.com. No lunch weekends. Bus: 50 to Roscoe. AE, D, DC, MC, V. $$–$$$

RESI'S BIERSTUBE This tavern's back yard, lantern-lit after dark, is one of Chicago's oldest and best beer gardens. Wurst plates are favorites, but schnitzel and goulash are also worthy 2034 W Irving Park Rd, between Seeley and Hoyne, 773/472-1749. No lunch. El: Brown to Irving Park. AE, MC, V. $

● **SOLA** Los Angeles native and self-professed surfer girl Carol Wallack opened this bright, open, contemporary restaurant with floor-to-ceiling windows. On the Asian-inspired menu, look for pork tenderloin with onion puree and candied bacon, miso black cod with bamboo rice and

curried sunchokes, and seared wasabi-crusted scallops with fava beans and avocado-blood orange sauce. 3868 N Lincoln Ave, betw Byron and Berenice, 773/327-3868, sola-restaurant.com. Also serves brunch weekends; no lunch Sat–Wed. El: Brown to Addison. AE, D, MC, V. $$–$$$

● **TERRAGUSTO** The small Italian menu at this sparc, comfortable café favors organic ingredients and Midwest beef and poultry. The simple but on-the-mark homemade pasta dishes include stracci (ragged pasta) with braised pork shoulder and Parmesan, and tagliatelle with Bolognese sauce. The roast free-range half chicken and pork rib chops are big enough to share. 1851 W Addison St, at Wolcott, 773/248-2777, terragustochicago.com. Closed Mon and Tues. BYOB. El: Brown to Addison. AE, D, MC, V. $$

● **VICTORY'S BANNER** This cheery vegetarian breakfast and lunch spot is staffed by the unfailingly pleasant meditation acolytes of spiritualist Sri Chinmoy. Oat-bran pancakes and buckwheat waffles come with maple syrup and fresh fruit, and all eggs are from free-range chickens. At lunch: salads, veggie burgers, and wraps. 2100 W Roscoe St, at Hoyne, 773/665-0227, victorysbanner.com. No dinner; closed Tues. El: Brown to Paulina. AE, D, DC, MC, V. $

WHERE TO EAT WHEREVER YOU ARE

LINCOLN SQUARE

Winnemac Park

W. WINNEMAC AVE.
W. ARGYLE ST.
W. WINNEMAC AVE.

N. LINCOLN AVE.
N. WESTERN AVE.
N. CLAREMONT AVE.
N. OAKLEY AVE.
N. BELL AVE.
N. LEAVITT ST.
N. HAMILTON AVE.
N. HOYNE AVE.
N. SEELEY AVE.
N. DAMEN AVE.
N. WINCHESTER AVE.
N. WOLCOTT AVE.

W. LAWRENCE AVE.
W. LAWRENCE AVE.

Pizza D.O.C.
W. GIDDINGS ST.

Chicago Brauhaus
Café Selmarie
W. LELAND AVE.

N. RAVENSWOOD AVE.
N. HERMITAGE AVE.

Opart Thai House
W. EASTWOOD AVE.
W. EASTWOOD AVE.
Spoon Thai
Fiddlehead Café
W. WILSON AVE.
W. WILSON AVE.

The Grafton
Bistro Campagne
Tank Sushi
Spacca Napoli

N. CAMPBELL AVE.
N. ARTESIAN AVE.
W. SUNNYSIDE AVE.

Welles Park

W. MONTROSE AVE.
W. MONTROSE AVE.

N. LINCOLN AVE.
N. WESTERN AVE.
W. CULLOM AVE.
N. DAMEN AVE.
N. WINCHESTER AVE.
N. WOLCOTT AVE.

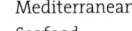

- American
- Chinese
- European
- Italian
- Japanese
- French and Contemporary
- Latin
- Mediterranean
- Seafood
- Steak
- World

● **BISTRO CAMPAGNE** This relaxed bistro in Lincoln Square stands out for its menu full of well-executed classics like roast chicken, grilled salmon with lentils, escargots, and steak *frites* (steak and fries). And the garden is idyllic in summer.
4518 N Lincoln Ave, betw Wilson and Sunnyside, 773/271-6100, bistrocampagne.com. El: Brown to Western. AE, MC, V.
$$–$$$

● **CAFÉ SELMARIE** This former bakery now serves three meals a day. For breakfast, it's not just farm-fresh eggs—you can also get croissant French toast flavored with Triple Sec and steel-cut Irish oatmeal with date-nut butter. At lunch, there are soups, wraps, and sandwiches (say, smoked turkey and Brie), and dinner adds panko-crusted tilapia and Hungarian goulash. The house macaroni and cheese is made with leeks and four cheeses. There's outdoor seating on the plaza.
4729 N Lincoln Ave, at Giddings, 773/989-9595, cafeselmarie.com. Also serves breakfast daily and brunch Sun; no lunch Sun. El: Brown to Western. MC, V.
$–$$

● **CHICAGO BRAUHAUS** Traditional European sauerbraten, Wiener schnitzel, boiled pork shank, and other dishes fill the menu at this restaurant—you could be in Austria. The selection of imported beer and wine is extensive, and there's nightly live music and dancing from the Brauhaus Trio.
4732 N Lincoln Ave, at Giddings, chicagobrauhaus.com, 773/784-4444. Closed Tues. El: Brown to Western. AE, D, MC, V.
$$

● **FIDDLEHEAD CAFÉ** The menu at this bistro with a global twist begins with a dozen shareable appetizers—flatbread with truffle ricotta and arugula, and ahi tuna with tomato-pancetta jam, mussels with bacon, garlic, and sherry. Entrées are artfully conceived as well. But the real buzz is about the wine list, 350 bottles strong. You can order many wines by the glass or by the flight, to savor with selections from the equally robust cheese list. 4600 N Lincoln Ave, at Wilson, 773/751-1500, fiddleheadcafe.com. Also serves breakfast weekends; no lunch weekdays. El: Brown to Western. AE, D, MC, V.
$$

● **THE GRAFTON** Students from the nearby Old Town School of Folk Music stage impromptu music sessions

around the back-room fireplace at this comfortable, dark-oak-furnished Irish pub and grill. Standards like fish-and-chips, beef-and-Guinness stew, chili, shepherd's pie, and burgers round out the menu, and there's a nice selection of British and Irish beers on tap. 4530 N Lincoln Ave, betw Sunnyside and Wilson, 773/271-9000, thegrafton .com. No lunch weekdays. El: Brown to Western. AE, D, MC, V.
$

● **OPART THAI HOUSE** Kudos go out to this Thai for its signature Tiger Cry (thin-sliced beef with spicy sauce) and for its garlic beef, pad thai, and *tom yum kai* (hot-and-sour soup with lemongrass, and mushrooms). Noodles rice, and curries round out the menu. 4658 N Western Ave, betw Leland and Eastwood, 773/989-8517, opartthai .com. BYOB. El: Brown to Western. AE, D, DC, MC, V.
$

● **PIZZA D.O.C.** Pizza here is Roman style, as 12-inch pies cooked in a wood-fired oven, in more than 20 varieties. On weekends, the dining room is crowded but there's plenty of room for all. 2251 W Lawrence Ave, betw Bell and Oakley, 773/784-8777, pizza-doc.com. No lunch weekdays. El: Brown to Western. AE, D, MC, V.
$$

● **SPACCA NAPOLI** A mosaic tiled wood fired oven constructed on-site by Neapolitan craftspeople is the focal point of this restaurant and the source of the pliable, blackened-crust, Neapolitan-style pizzas here. Starters are worthy, too—eggplant, zucchini, or prosciutto with arugula.
1769 W Sunnyside, at Ravenswood, 773/878-2420, spaccanapolipizzeria.com. Closed Mon and Tues. El: Brown to Montrose. AE, D, MC, V.
$

● **SPOON THAI** Of Lincoln Square's many Thais, this storefront stands out, offering an authentic experience at modest prices. Banana-blossom salad with chicken tossed in coconut milk is popular; fried chicken and panang curry with beef are also good options.
4608 N Western Ave, betw Wilson and Eastwood, 773/769-1173. El: Brown to Western. MC, V.
$

● **TANK SUSHI** Delectable small and large plates such as firecracker shrimp wrapped in wontons, tofu breaded with *panko* (Japanese breadcrumbs), and Szechuan pepper-crusted New York strip steak with tempura mushrooms make this sleek, stylish Lincoln Square sushi hangout stand out from the raw-fish crowd. In addition to a standard selection of *nigiri* (thin slices of raw fish on rice), Tank has its own tempting *maki* (with fish, rice, and other ingredients wrapped in dried seaweed): The Latin Heat combines smoked salmon with jalapeños, avocado, and chili mayo, and the Green Island pairs albacore with shiitake mushrooms, spicy coconut mayo, sesame seeds, and seaweed.
4514 N Lincoln Ave, betw Sunnyside and Wilson, 773/769-2600, tanksushi.com. No lunch weekdays. El: Brown to Western. AE, D, MC, V.
$$$

UPTOWN AND ANDERSONVILLE

- American
- Chinese
- European
- Italian
- Japanese
- French and Contemporary
- Latin
- Mediterranean
- Seafood
- Steak
- World

● **AGAMI** This Japanese has a stylish black-and-red color scheme, painted concrete floors, and eight private booths that beckon behind flowing curtains The menu lists maki like the Agami—with lightly battered spicy tuna, cream cheese, shrimp, avocado, and asparagus—plus a sashimi list and spontaneous creations whipped up by chef Soon Park.
4712 N Broadway St, at Leland, 773/506-1854. No lunch. El: Red to Lawrence. AE, D, MC, V.
$$–$$$

● **ANDIES RESTAURANT** This bustling storefront diner serves Lebanese and Greek cuisine at reasonable prices. Lentil soup, spinach-stuffed artichokes, vegetarian moussaka, and various kabobs are among the menu highlights.
5253 N Clark St, betw Farragut and Berwyn, 773/784-8616, andiesres.com. Bus: 22 to Berwyn. AE, D, MC, V.
$$

● **CAFÉ HOANG** Located in the heart of Chicago's Vietnamese community, this storefront serves Vietnamese and Thai dishes—a spicy chicken salad loaded with chicken, peanuts, and red peppers; stir-fried meats with steamed rice; big bowls of soup. BYOB.
1010 W Argyle St, betw Kenmore and Sheridan, 773/878-9943. Closed Tues. El: Red to Argyle. AE, MC, V.
$

● **HAI YEN** If the huge Chinese and Vietnamese menu overwhelms you, the friendly staff will help you choose among noodle, poultry, beef, fish, and rice dishes or steer you to fun tabletop fondue, soup pot, and grill options.
1055 W Argyle St, betw Kenmore and Winthrop, 773/561-4077, haiyen restaurant.com. Closed Wed. El: Red to Argyle. MC, V.
$

● **HAMBURGER MARY'S** Fun burgers, sandwiches, pizzas, and salads are served with campy flair at this Andersonville location decked with kitschy artwork and boldly painted walls. Food is served until 11 pm.
5400 N Clark St, at Balmoral, 773/784-6969, hamburgermaryschicago.com. Bus: 22 to Balmoral. AE, D, MC, V.
$–$$

● **HOPLEAF** Once a small tavern, Hopleaf has grown. But the focus remains on the beer: 24 on tap, including Belgian ales and U.S. microbrews. The great bar food includes mussels steamed in Wittekerke ale, Belgian-style meatballs, and serious entrées like organic rib-eye steak. A jazz jukebox and European-beer posters add character.
5148 N Clark St, at Foster, 773/334-9851, hopleaf.com. No lunch. Bus: 22 to Foster. AE, D, DC, MC, V.
$$

● **JIN JU** Sleek and hip, with a mellow soundtrack, this is not your typical Korean. For the uninitiated, though, it's a great spot to discover Korean dishes like bi bim bop (rice topped with beef, vegetables, and a fried egg) or kalbi (beef short ribs), for instance.
5203 N Clark St, at Foster, 773/334-6377. Closed Mon; no lunch. Bus: 22 to Foster. AE, MC, V.
$$

● **KOPI CAFÉ** This cozy Clark Street spot has a backpacker vibe thanks to its travel-inspired theme: wall clocks showing the time in international cities, bookshelves stacked with travel books for sale, and a tiny Asian crafts and clothes boutique in the rear. The vegetarian menu lists café standards such as sandwiches, burritos, spinach pies, and a host of coffee and tea drinks.
5317 N Clark St, betw Summerdale and Berwyn, 773/989-5674. Also serves breakfast. Bus: 22 to Summerdale. AE, D, MC, V.
$

● **LA TACHE** Traditional French bistro fare is prepared with a creative twist at La Tache. Try the classic *brandade* (salt-cod puree) with tomato confit, a *croque monsieur* (toasted ham-and-cheese sandwich), or steak *frites* (steak and fries) with a choice of garlic-anchovy butter, green-peppercorn sauce, or another sauce.
1475 W Balmoral Ave, betw Clark and Glenwood, 773/334-7168, latache chicago.com. Also serves brunch Sun; no lunch. Bus: 22 to Balmoral. AE, D, DC, MC, V.
$$–$$$

● **MARIGOLD** Gritty-but-gentrifying Uptown gets a modern Indian restaurant, complete with bold red and yellow walls, glittery mosaic tile, and a small, foodie-pleasing menu. Try the lamb vindaloo or the confit-style duck leg cured in Indian spices and served with stir-fried green beans.
4832 N Broadway St, betw Lawrence and Gunnison, 773/293-4653, marigoldrestaurant.com. No lunch; closed Mon. El: Red to Lawrence. AE, D, DC, MC, V.
$$

● **OLÉ OLÉ** Exposed brick walls and front windows that flood the storefront space with light are decorative highlights of this cool, urban Latin hangout. The numerous small and large plates on the menu run from ceviche and empanadas to fire-grilled squid, shrimp fajitas, arroz con pollo, and carne asada.
5413 N Clark St, betw Rascher and Balmoral, 773/293-2222. No lunch. Bus: 22 to Balmoral. AE, D, DC, MC, V.
$$

● **REZA'S** The lofty and bright main dining room at this vegetarian-friendly Persian restaurant draws a diverse crowd that comes for large platters of chicken, beef, and fish kebabs served with dilled rice and grilled peppers, tomatoes, and onions. Start with the vegetarian appetizer sampler, which includes hummus, tabouli, dolmeh (stuffed grape leaves and peppers), falafel, and kashkeh bodemjan, a dip made of eggplant, curds, and whey.
5255 N Clark St, at Berwyn, 773/561-1898, rezasrestaurant.com. Bus: 22 to Berwyn. AE, D, DC, MC, V.
$

● **SWEDISH BAKERY** In a perfect world, every neighborhood would have a bakery like this Andersonville institution, where specialty breads are baked on different days of the week—cracked wheat on Monday, cranberry-walnut-raisin on Wednesday—and every possible variation of cookie, cake, pie, torte, and petit four tempts visitors from behind the counter. This carryout-only bakery is usually busy, but the line moves efficiently.
5348 N Clark St, betw Summerdale and Balmoral, 773/561-8919, swedishbakery.com. Closed Sun. Bus: 22 to Summerdale. AE, D, DC, MC, V.
$

● **TANK NOODLE** The menu at this bright, friendly Vietnamese restaurant is expansive and a bit unwieldy, but newcomers to the cuisine can ask for guidance. The main dish is pho—beef broth poured over noodles and vegetables—and it's prepared here with endless variations. Other rice and noodle dishes are served with plates of spices, to allow everyone to season to his or her own taste.
4955 N Broadway St, at Argyle, 773/878-2253, tanknoodle.com. Also serves breakfast; closed Wed. El: Red to Argyle. D, MC, V.
$

● **TWEET** This American nook takes a contemporary approach to homey fare made with organic ingredients .Go for buckwheat pancakes, biscuits and gravy, and crab cakes with hollandaise. An ATM is on-site.s
5020 N Sheridan Rd, betw Carmen and Argyle, 773/728-5576, tweet.biz. Also serves breakfast; no lunch; closed Tues. El: Red to Argyle. Bus: 151 to Argyle. No credit cards.
$$

INDEX

A

Adesso 73
Agami 87
Al's #1 Italian Beef 12, 57
Alinea 4
Alinea 67
Andie's Restaurant 87
Ann Sather 73
Ashkenaz Delicatessen 31
Asian Top Picks 10-11
Athena 49
Athenian Room 67
Atwood Café 41
Avec 49
Avenues 4, 21

B

Ben Pao 21
Bice Ristorante 22
Billy Goat 16, 22
Bin 36, 22
Bin Wine Café 61
Bistro 110 31
Bistro Campagne 83
Bittersweet 73
Blackbird 50
Blue Fin 61
Bombon 8, 57
Brasserie Jo 23
Bravo Tapas and
    Lounge 62
Bucktown and Wicker
    Park restaurants 60-65

C

Café Absinthe 62
Café Ba-Ba-Reeba! 68
Café des Architectes 31
Café Hoang 88
Café Iberico 37
Café Selmarie 14, 83
Café 28 79
Cape Cod Room 32
Capital Grille 23
Carnivale 8, 45
Carson's 37
Charlie Trotter's 4, 68
Charlie's Ale House 68
Cheap Chow Top
    Picks 12-13
Chicago Brauhaus 83
Chicago Chop House 23
Chicago Diner 74
Chicago Firehouse
    Restaurant 53
Cho Sun Ok 79
Coco Pazzo 37
Coobah 74
Costa's 50
credit cards 3
Cru Café and Wine Bar 32
Cuernavaca 8, 57

D

D'Agostino's 74
Delacosta 23
Deleece 74
Diner Grill 12, 79
Dinotto Ristorante 32

Ditka's Restaurant 32
Duke of Perth 74

E

Earwax 16, 62
Erwin 75
Everest 41
Extra Virgin 45

F

Fan Si Pan 45
Fiddlehead Café 84
Fireplace Inn 33
Fixture 69
Flatwater 14, 37
Fogo de Chão 38
Foodlife 12
Foodlife 33
404 Wine Bar 75
Fox & Obel 24
French and Contempo-
    rary Top Picks 4-5
Frontera Grill/
    Topolobampo 9, 24

G

Gene and Georgetti 38
Gibsons Steakhouse 33
Gino's East, The
    Original 24
Gioco 53
Gold Coast and Old
    Town 30-35
Goose Island Beer Co. 69
Greek Islands 50

Greektown and West Loop areas restaurant 48–51
Green Dolphin Street 69
Green Door Tavern 38
Green Zebra 45

H
Habana Libre 46
Hai Yen 10, 88
Hamburger Mary's 88
Harmony Grill 75
Harry Caray's 25
Hema's Kitchen 69
Hopleaf 17, 88
Hugo's Frog Bar & Fish House 33

I
Indian Garden 25
Intelligentsia Coffee 75
Italian and Pizza Top Picks 6–7
Italian Village 41

J
Jack's On Halsted 76
Japonais 38
Jin Ju 88
Julius Meinl 76

K
Kamehachi 33
Kaze Sushi 80
Kiki's Bistro 38
Kit Kat Lounge & Supper Club 76

Kopi Café 89

L
La Tache 89
La Tavernetta 77
Lakeview restaurants 72–77
Lao Sze Chuan 10, 53
Laschet's Inn 80
Latin Top Picks 8–9
Lawry's The Prime Rib 26
Le Colonial 34
Le Lan 10, 26
Lincoln Park area restaurants 66–71
Lincoln Square area restaurants 82–85
Local Favorites Top Picks 16–17
Loop area restaurants 40–43
Lou Malnati's 39
Lou Mitchell's 51
Luna Caprese 70

M
Macy's Walnut Room 17, 42
Magnificent Mile and Streeterville restaurants 20–29
Mambo Grill 34
Manny's Coffee Ship & Deli 54
Marché 46
Marigold 11, 90

Mas 9, 63
May Street Café 58
Meritage 63
Mia Francesca 6, 77
Milk & Honey Café 63
Miller's Pub 42
Moto 5, 46
Mrs. Murphy & Sons Irish Bistro 80
Mulan 54
Mundial-Cocina Mestiza 58

N
Nacional 27 9, 39
Nick's Fishmarket & Grill 42
Nick's Pit Stop 63
Nomi 14, 34
North Pond 70
Northside Bar and Grill 15, 64
Nueva Léon 13, 58

O
Oasis Café 42
Olé Olé 90
One Sixtyblue 47
Opart Thai House 84
Opera 54
Outdoor Dining Top Picks 14–15
Oysy 26

P

Palm Court 34
Perry's Deli 43
Phil Stefani's 437
Phoenix Restaurant 55
Piazza Bella Trattoria 80
Pilsen and Little Italy
 restaurants 56-59
Pizza D.O.C. 84
Pizzeria Uno 6, 27
Podhalanka Polksa
 Restauracja 13, 64
Portillo's Hot Dogs 39
Potbelly Sandwich
 Works 70
price categories 3

R

R.J. Grunts 71
Randolph Market and
 River West areas
 restaurants 44-47
Red Lion Pub 71
Redfish 27
Resi's Bierstube 15, 80
Reza's 90
Rhapsody 43
Riva 28
River North area
 restaurants 36-39
Roscoe Village and
 North Center area
 restaurants 78-81
Rush 27
Russian Tea Time 43

S

Salpicón 34
Sapori 17, 71
Schwa 64
Scylla 65
17/West at the
 Berghoff 13, 43
Shanghai Terrace 28
Shaw's Crab House 28
Signature Room at the
 95th 5, 34
Silver Cloud Bar &
 Grill 65
Singha 28
676 Restaurant 29
Skylark 58 Sola 81
South Loop and
 Chinatown 52-55
Spacca Napoli 6, 85
Spiaggia 7, 35
Spoon 34
Spoon Thai 85
Sushi Wabi 47
Swedish Bakery 91

T

Tango Sur 77
Tank Noodle 91
Tank Sushi 11, 85
Tavern On Rush 35
Terragusto 7, 81
Thai Classic 11, 77
The Grafton 84
The Kerry Man 25
The Smoke Daddy 65
Three Happiness
 Restaurant 55

Timo 15, 47
Toast 71
Top Picks 4-17
Trattoria No. 10 43
Tru 5, 29
Tufano's Vernon Park
 Tap 7, 59
Tuscany 59
Tweet 91
Twin Anchors 35

U

Uptown and Anderson-
 ville restaurants 86-91

V

Venus Greek-Cypriot
 Cuisine 51
Vermillion 29
Victory's Banner 81
VTK 29

W

West Town Tavern 47
Wildfire 39
Wishbone 47

Y

Yoshi's Café 77

Z

Zapatista 55

WHERE > CHICAGO > EAT!
Editor: Deborah Kaufman
Writing: John McLaughlin; J.P. Anderson, Editor, and Elisa Drake, Associate Editor, and the editors of Where® magazine
Other contributors: Karen Ingebretson, Kristin Smith
Fact-checking: Susan Cosley

Photography: Joe Viesti
Cover and interior design: Georgiana Goodwin
Map design: PopOut maps originally designed and produced by CM Cartographics
Maps: Tim Kissel

Acknowledgments
Thanks to the many restaurateurs who provided assistance to the writers and photographer, and to Jet Blue, which flies travelers to the Windy City in leather-seated comfort from more than 50 cities nationwide.

Important Advice
Always reserve ahead, or at least phone to make sure a restaurant will be serving when you show up. We've worked hard to make the text and maps accurate, but cities change fast, and it's better to be safe than sorry.

Copyright
Text copyright © 2008 Morris Book Publishing, LLC
PopOut map copyright © 2008 Compass Map, Ltd.
Interior maps © 2008 Morris Book Publishing, LLC.

Where is a registered trademark of Morris Visitor Publications.
PopOut is a trademark of Compass Map, Ltd.

popout™map, popout™cityguide, and associated products are the subject of patents pending worldwide.

All rights reserved. No part of this book may be reproduced or transmitted in any form by any means, electronic or mechanical, including photocopying and recording, or by any information storage and retrieval system, except as may be expressly permitted by the 1976 Copyright Act or by the publisher. Requests for permission should be made in writing to The Globe Pequot Press, P.O. Box 480, Guilford, Connecticut 06437.

Photo Credits
All photographs © Joe Viesti/Viestiphoto.com except for the following pages: 4 and 67l courtesy of Alinea, 6t and 77 courtesy of Francesca Restaurants, 9t photo by Tim Turner, 14b courtesy of Nomi Restaurant, 15t courtesy of Northside Bar & Grill, 15m photo by John McLaughlin, 23 courtesy of Capital Grille, 46r courtesy of Moto restaurant, 70 courtesy of Potbelly Sandwich Works, 76 courtesy of Kit Kat Lounge, 91t photo provided by Swedish Bakery. Also, from Shutterstock: title page © Denis Miraniuk, 2-3 © Dariusz Sas, 9b © hd connelly, 18-19 © Condor 36, 24 © trialart-info, 38 © Chris Bence, 50 © Brett Mulcany, 75 ©MW, 91b © Elena Schweitzer.

Library of Congress Cataloging-in-Publication Data is available.

ISBN 978-0-7627-4626-2

Manufactured in China
First Edition/First Printing

Where QuickGuide

Where PopOut Map & Guide

Where Magazine

Where Guestbook

Your Travel Portfolio™